# CAN'T BE ARSED

RICHARD WILSON

# CAN'T BE ARSED

## ARSED

### 101 THINGS **NOT** TO DO
### BEFORE YOU DIE

**PORTICO**

First published in the United Kingdom in 2008 by
Portico Books
10 Southcombe Street
London
W14 0RA

An imprint of Anova Books Company Ltd

ISBN 978-1-906032-93-7

A CIP catalogue record for this book is available from the British Library.

11 12 13 14 15 16 17 18 19

Printed and bound by 1010 Printing International Ltd, China

Illustrations by Jack Noel

This book can be ordered direct from the publisher at www.anovabooks.com

# Contents

● ● ● ● ● ● ● ● ● ● ● ● ● ● ● ● ● ● ● ● ● ● ● ● ● ● ● ● ● ● ● ● ● ● ● ● ● ● ● ●

## CULTURAL SECTION

### Albums

## Films

## Books

If you really can't be arsed to read the whole book, this Venn diagram will give you a pretty good idea of what's in it.

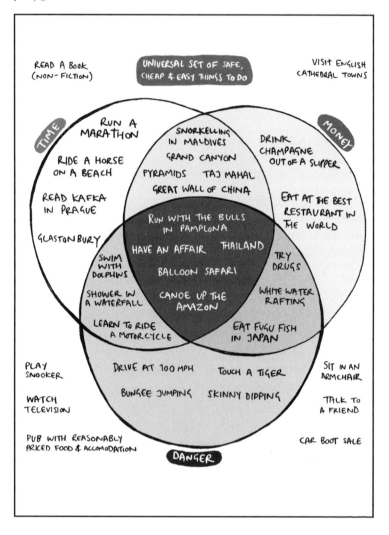

# Introduction

• • • • • • • • • • • • • • • • • • • • • • • • • • • • • • • •

You might think from the title of this book that it's some kind of Slacker's Manifesto – a manual for the apathetic, advocating diffidence, disinterest, lethargy and general lounging around doing bugger all. Well in a way it is, but there's more to it than that. There's something about the zeal of those who chase around the world in a desperate search for awesome 'once in a lifetime' experiences that demands a much more positive negative reaction than mere apathy.

*Can't Be Arsed* is a counterblast to those self-satisfied tossers who regard their own life as a compilation of greatest hits. No room for flops – everything has to be brilliant; nothing can be just OK. 'Life's too short,' they say as if they are the only ones who understand mortality, and yet they squander their own three score-years-and-ten by desperately trying to cram as many quarts as possible into their pint pot.

If they kept it to themselves it wouldn't bother me, but no; they are constantly ordering the rest of us around with their books and blogs and newspaper articles and collections of holiday snaps, warning us that life is passing us by and that there are 1,001 things in 1,001 categories which must be seen and done before we die. Presumably, when we've done them all, we're supposed to reach for the nearest revolver and blow our own brains out.

The worst of these evangelistic thrill-seekers congregate on the internet, where they fiddle with their hideous creation, the 'to do list'. It's normally a collection of a hundred and one things to experience before you're thirty, or fifty or dead, and it contains a variety of predictable travel destinations, death-defying stunts and New Age crap. Infuriating comments are posted by people who are seriously trying to tick off the entire list, such as: 'I've just completed my 43rd (Smoke a peace-pipe with a Native American). How many have you done?'

We should resist this challenge. Knock the monitor off the desk and smash it to bits in a rage, yes – but resist the challenge. We don't have to go anywhere, buy anything, watch anything, listen to anything, inhale anything, smoke any kind of peace-pipe with anyone or insert anything anywhere we don't want. We can sit in an armchair and stare into space all afternoon if we like, we can potter around agreeable market towns within an hour's drive of where we live, if the mood takes us.

To anyone who urges awesome, life-enhancing, never-to-be-repeated experiences upon us, *Can't Be Arsed* is the perfect riposte. It conveys just the right amount of ignorance and narrow-mindedness to drive them round the bend. But there is no ignorance here – I think we know exactly what these people are trying to do.

Travellers are the worst. Not holidaymakers you understand, but 'travellers'. Travel is the compartment of our lives that we are supposed to cram so full of experiences that it's bursting at the seams. My passport should have more visa stamps in it than Carlos The Jackal's; I should have more exotic photos on my hard drive than Gary Glitter.

The gap year is to blame for all this. When did that start? When did it become acceptable for young people to piss about for a whole year in a foreign country, before pissing about for three years at university? A whole year to fritter away Mummy and Daddy's money in search of life-expanding experiences and exotic, hitherto-unimagined brushes with death!

Not surprisingly, the freedom of these feckless pre-students created a jealous globetrotting frenzy in older couples, feeling cheated of a privileged youth; then people who had only been at work for a couple of years since leaving university started poncing off to 'go travelling' (doesn't anybody do any work?). Now we have an entire branch of the travel industry devoted to excursions and adventures abroad that no one in their right mind would call a proper holiday.

But when anyone recommends a spectacular/exotic/life-enhancing travel destination to me, my immediate reaction is: it's too far away, too dangerous or too expensive. As a Yorkshireman, meanness and caution come naturally to me. But I don't want to give the impression that this outlook is only the preserve of someone who is lucky enough to be born there. Many people have said that Yorkshire isn't a place, it's an attitude of mind. Anyone can have it if they really try. In fact, the Yorkshire outlook has been around for thousands of years. The Platonists, Stoics, Christians, Muslims, Jews and Buddhists all share the knowledge of this fundamental truth – that happiness is not about achieving or having or seeing as much as possible. Yes, happiness *is* about getting what you want, but the key is not wanting much in the first place. Reduce your desires, lower your expectations and expect the worst. Above all, be careful what you wish for – it might be a bit rubbish.

This blinkered view is very much underrated.

My father-in-law, also from Yorkshire, has developed a sure-fire way of enjoying every meal: without fail he has chips, peas and some form of grilled meat. Always. He explains it like this: 'There is a good enough range of simple English food you can eat, without risking an upset stomach for the sake of experimentation. It's like cricket – if you can't play the hook shot, don't play it – you'll get yourself out.'

You could say he can't be arsed to try anything new, but I say he has found the road to Shangri-La.

In the same way we should reject the cultural imperialism of the broad-minded who are forever suggesting new experiences, be they musical, cinematic, sensual, spiritual or gastronomic – 1,001 albums you must hear before you die, 1,001 films you must see before you die, 1,001 paintings you must see before you die, this year's must-have handbag, Thai salmon fishcakes to die for. There is simply too much choice and too many people making recommendations. It's a lot of effort, a lot of expense and, at the end of the day, we might not like it.

This book has a list of the kind of things that dangerously broadminded and adventurous people will try and persuade you to do on the grounds that you might die in the next forty years. Maybe it will help you to shrug off their taunts. Because yes, people will call you boring, or a stick-in-the-mud, or a miserable Yorkshire bastard, but remember this: there's nothing more boring than someone else's holiday snaps, or their tales of how drunk they were on Saturday or how much bondage has improved their sex life. Someone once said that the most boring thing in the world is other people's dreams, but at least they don't have boring dreams on purpose; some people actually *choose* to go Uruguay.

The list is in a sort of order but I couldn't be arsed to work out what goes in which category, or even what the categories are, however all the examples are taken from genuine lists of things to do before you die on the Internet or in published books. In the spirit of *Can't Be Arsed*, do feel free to ignore my selection and avoid doing a completely different list of things altogether . . .

# Visit Machu Picchu

● ● ● ● ● ● ● ● ● ● ● ● ● ● ● ● ● ● ● ● ● ● ● ● ● ● ● ● ● ● ● ●

Machu Picchu, in deepest Peru, is one of the top sights you're to supposed to see before you snuff it. Fair enough, it looks fantastic.

But hang on, though - it's 6,000 miles away. That's twelve thrombotic hours on a plane followed by a bladder-busting seven-hour bus ride. However great the view at the end of it, there's no way it can be worth that kind of torture; that's if you can see anything at all through the throngs of gap-year gits jostling you with their stupid rucksacks and murmuring the internationally approved expression of appreciation - 'totally awesome, dude!' They'll all be taking exactly the same picture. This is it:

It's supposed to be the face of a noble Inca, lying on his back gazing at the stars, but to me it looks more like Bruce Forsyth having a nap.

Didn't they do well, those Incas?

Actually, I like the photographs. I also liked Michael Palin's TV programme about it and, for me, that's good enough. How does going there make it any better? Ironically, the number of tourists (or travellers as they like to be known) has dramatically increased since Palin declared it his favourite place in all the world. And this ever growing number of tourists/travellers/tossers who make the trip each year pose the greatest threat to the area's integrity, wearing away footpaths and knocking walls over. Another example of evil Westerners spoiling a native paradise, just like those horrible Conquistadors 500 years ago.

Maybe this is why Machu Picchu has such an attraction for some people. It's a spectacular, awe-inspiring guilt-trip. These people are like Charlton Heston in Planet of the Apes. His horse rounds the cliff and he sees the Statue of Liberty buried up to the waist in sand and he cries: 'You maniacs! You blew it up!! Damn you! God damn you all to hell!!!'

OK, they don't say that exactly, but I've no doubt many a wistful backpacker has moaned that "We've like totally destroyed this civilisation. We could have learned so much from them!'

Well, we did learn something from them. We learned about cocaine – the drug of choice for wankers everywhere. The Spanish brought the Incas' favourite leaf back to Europe and laid the foundation for an industry which damages countryside, brings misery and fear to local farmers, and litters the fields that children play in with land mines; merely trafficking the drug kills untold thousands every year, not to mention the millions of individuals who have been bored senseless at parties by coked-up jerks and their plans for world domination. So you can see all the trouble a little taste for travel and adventure can bring. Best stay at home, eh?

# Canoe up the Amazon

Water-based transport really appeals to me. I love boats – car ferries, cabin cruisers, barges, anything that goes slowly and requires little or no effort (so not yachts – and actually, come to think of it, barges can be a bugger with those locks and everything). I very much prefer my water transport to be on an English river or at worst crossing the Channel or the Irish Sea. So paddling a canoe through the South American jungle doesn't hold the same attraction.

The main drawback for me, apart from the location and the canoeing bit, is the water of the Amazon itself and, more specifically, what it contains: the candiru fish. Every man knows about this – an evil bastard of a fish that deliberately seeks out the penis, so it can swim up it and shoot out spines that embed themselves inside the urethra. These fish can grow up to six inches long – that's right: six extremely painful inches long. It's impossible to remove without surgery*, which involves slicing open the penis like an Arbroath Smokie and gouging the devil out. I heard this from a mate of mine who knows a nurse, so it's definitely true. Should you be careless enough to urinate in the water these fish can detect you from miles away and follow the wee trail right up your old chap. I don't know if it's the same for women, but either way, hardly worth the risk, is it?

*There is a local Amazonian remedy that apparently involves inserting an entire apple into the affected area. Not what you'd call a painless alternative.

# Shower in a Waterfall

People who dream of doing this probably imagine it will be exactly like that Timotei shampoo ad, in which an impossibly beautiful blonde girl washes her already-quite-clean hair in a waterfall and then flicks her golden tresses this way and that, in super slow-mo.

It all looks so tempting, refreshing, natural and clean. But remember, this is advertising! It's all faked. The film has been tinkered with – it's never *that* sunny – the water has been dyed blue, the shampoo is Gale's Honey, the girl's in a cage in a wetsuit. It's not her hair, they used a stunt hair double, or it's made of mashed potato and Plasticine; she's not really there, there is no waterfall, she's a mannequin, it's all done in a studio in Elstree and we don't actually exist – we're a figment in the mind of a silicon-based life form who sits at a desk in an office in Clerkenwell.

There is supposed to be a real-life waterfall like the one in the Timotei ad, in a place called Millaa Millaa in Queensland, Australia. I don't actually believe this – the ad men must have made it up. But it doesn't matter which waterfall you try to shower in; you'll be freezing cold and your thighs will go all blue and blotchy. Not only that, but you'll have left the soap or the shampoo in your rucksack and you'll have to step out of the shower to get it and then in the process you'll probably slip on some moss or slime and crack your elbow, maybe end up with a couple of

10

grazed shins and skinned ankles. And after all that, you'll find that one of your 'mad' travelling companions has stolen your clothes for a joke then videoed you on their mobile and by the time you've attempted to dry yourself on some leaves (causing a rather alarming burning sensation) your wobbling bulk is being viewed worldwide on YouTube. Now *that* could happen.

# See the Great Wall of China

● ● ● ● ● ● ● ● ● ● ● ● ● ● ● ● ● ● ● ● ● ● ● ● ● ● ● ● ● ● ● ● ●

It's a toss-up as to who's more annoying: the people who say 'it's visible from space, you know' or the people who say 'you know, of course, it's a myth that it's visible from space'.

Well, I do know that the Great Wall of China's at least 4,000 miles long, so if you're not in space, you'll never see all of it. If you did drag yourself out there you'd probably be able to take in a few miles of wall dotted with some forts; all impressive enough, but it's like trying to take a photograph of a fireworks display – you can try to get it all in but you never will. What's more, it's in China. Why would anyone want to go *there*?

Let's be honest, the Chinese force women to have abortions, they drive tanks over students, they shoot monks, they execute prisoners in mobile lethal-injection vans and they eat tigers. And whatever else you might see on TV about China's exploding economy with a new power station completed every six days, the world's biggest airport and skyscrapers shooting up everywhere, the truth is its people are being sucked out of the countryside and shredded by the Industrial Machine like pork in a wan-ton.

Its cities are so jammed full of people looking for work that China has become a living Dickens novel. Behind every new office block there's a Cratchett family of sixty kids in a hovel, going blind by making knock-off *Star Wars* toys by candlelight. The BBC could save a fortune on costume-drama adaptations (and reduce our licence fee in the process) by just pointing a camera down the alleyways and gutters of Beijing. Of course, they wouldn't dare do that because in seconds a couple of Chinese policemen would turn up to arrest the film crew and deliver a sound beating to any local resident foolish enough to allow themselves to be filmed.

# Go to Thailand

My advice to anyone about to travel to Thailand is simple. Before you go, sort out a decent photo of yourself, preferably taken at a party smiling and laughing and celebrating the sheer joy of being alive. Why? Because the newspapers and TV news bulletins will want something to accompany the article about your tragic death: 'Horror in paradise . . . she was so happy-go-lucky . . . a flame that will never die . . .' Far better to go out in a photographic style of your choosing than leave it to some shitbag from school to flog syndication rights to that class photo when you were sixteen.

You have to take your straw hat off to Thailand, there are so many different ways it can kill you. There's all the obvious Southeast Asia stuff – malaria, dengue fever, Japanese encephalitis (sounds nice) and bird flu. A lot of scaremongering goes on about bird flu coming to Britain but I reckon you're far more likely to pick up a bit of H5N1 if you holiday in a country where chickens are kept in the lounge. Then, of course, there's the king of the natural disaster, the tsunami. Big ones only happen once every twelve years or so, but the locals will probably say that's enough.

But Thailand really punches above its weight is when it comes to man-made deaths. What a glorious array of people there is to be murdered by! Sex-crazed fishermen, jealous fellow backpackers, homicidal drifters, the pissed-up landlords of 'hostels', trigger-happy policemen and malevolent cellmates in the prison you could find yourself in, following a doomed attempt at drug smuggling.

Over the last 25 years the number of attacks, murders, rapes and robberies against tourists is running well into the thousands. It seems that the kind of person who is attracted to this dreamy paradise of palm-fringed beaches and cocktails in coconuts is exactly the type to drop their guard in the presence of a devious and psychopathic local.

So what's Thailand got going for it?

It has beautiful beaches and great food; it's sunny and it's cheap. Then again, so is Torquay. Although I imagine Torquay has nothing on Thailand when it comes to top-quality ladyboys, hard-core porn and a booming child-sex industry. You wouldn't catch Gary Glitter on an under-age sex holiday in Torquay, would you?

One other great statistic you won't find in the tourist brochures is that Thailand is the number-one destination for motorcycle enthusiasts. Crash helmets are not compulsory and free spirits can zip around all over the country, unencumbered by any sweaty, uncomfortable headgear. It's risky, but as our intrepid travellers just love to say, 'If you don't take risks you'll never enjoy life to the full.' Quite right. And there are only 38 motorbike deaths a week in Thailand, so go on, live a little. Very little . . .

# Swim with Dolphins

This is on *every* list of things you simply must do before you die. 'It's sooo amaaaaazing.'

What? Having a randy, slimy, big-nosed mammal rub itself against you for sexual gratification? Because that's what they do you know – they try and encourage humans to masturbate them. It's common knowledge. 'Flogging the Dolphin' is even used as slang by some people for spilling one's seed on the ground, according to the Internet-based Urban Dictionary (although 'Internet-based' is also slang for 'totally made up').

And in 1991, a Manchester man was charged with masturbating a dolphin off the coast of Northumberland, so that the dolphin would prefer him to other swimmers. He was acquitted because the testimony of his accuser was deemed to be motivated by jealousy as *he* had been training dolphins to rip bikini tops off female swimmers. So not only are the dolphins dodgy, the people who swim with them are dodgy too.

Communing with dolphins is so fantastic, we're told, because they are highly intelligent. But are they, though? Now a dog, *that's* a smart animal. Sheep-herding, sniffing out drugs, disco dancing – one dog even made it to the finals of *Britain's Got Talent*. Do you think if Dolphins were that clever some TV people wouldn't have come up with a format for them by now?

Ok, so Dolphins have got this special language, which basically amounts to a lot of clicking noises like the ones you hear in the backing vocals on Kate Bush albums. But if they're so smart, why then don't dolphins warn each other that those metal things the US Navy keep strapping to their heads are in fact anti-submarine mines?

'*Click click.*'

(Not seen Flipper since that thing was strapped to his head.)

'*Click click, click click.*'

(Yes. Although I did hear a loud bang the other day and isn't that a bit of his tail floating in the water?)

I'm pretty sure conversations like this never happen, which proves my point.

I know we all feel guilty about killing dolphins through our deep love of tinned tuna, but flattering them with exaggerated estimations of their intelligence and trying to hang out with them while they're cruising the waterways in search of hand-relief isn't going to make the situation any better and, frankly, it makes us humans – the really intelligent beings on this planet – look a bit stupid.

# See the Taj Mahal

• • • • • • • • • • • • • • • • • • • • • • • • • • • • • • • • • • •

OK, it's a wonderful building. 'An eternal teardrop on the cheek of time', as Tagore put it. It was built as a memorial to Mumtaz, a devoted wife of Shah Jahan. He was so much in love with her he didn't bother having sex with any of his other wives. As a result she had thirteen children and while giving birth to the fourteenth, she died. So, the Taj Mahal is a shrine to the perfect, self-sacrificing devoted wife – a natural place for Princess Diana to be photographed, then.

Apart from the Taj Mahal's ingenious design and construction, its marble-clad surfaces appear to change colour, according to the light and time of day. I've actually been there and I can't fault it as a thing to look at, but then neither could I fault it in the photos I saw before I went there. And they didn't have loads of people like me taking pictures in the foreground.

You can never get to see the Taj Mahal as you imagine it to be. It will always be a disappointment – you'll psyche yourself up to be awestruck as you go through the gate and turn up to look at it for the first time. But it will be an anticlimax, no matter how much you kid yourself. We build things up far too much and – I hate to bang on about this – it's a heck of a way to go for an anticlimax. Nine hours on a plane to Delhi. Six hours on a train and then a half-mile struggle through the beggars and hawkers who await you at the station. On top of all that, it's bloody hot.

The typical tourist photo of the Taj Mahal is the square-on view with the pond in the foreground. It conveniently masks the Yamuna River behind it, one of the most polluted in the world, into which is dumped 57 per cent of New Delhi's waste. Maybe that's what Princess Diana could smell; something has to account for her moody expression in that famous picture. She went all the way to the Taj Mahal and sulked? She can't have thought it was that brilliant, then.

I'd just like to know, though, how she got her picture taken with no one else there? Privilege? No – I can't believe that even the Queen of People's Hearts could keep the foreground of the Taj Mahal empty for more than ten seconds before someone local crept in and tried to sell her some dyed cloth. Maybe her loyal flunkies in the tabloid press just airbrushed the people out;

or maybe she had herself Photoshopped in: Diana understood that the Taj Mahal is an image, not an experience.

I hate to base my judgement on actually having been there, but believe me, you'll lose nothing by not going.

# Go Snorkelling in the Maldives

● ● ● ● ● ● ● ● ● ● ● ● ● ● ● ● ● ● ● ● ● ● ● ● ● ● ● ● ● ● ● ●

This is slightly tautological as there is bugger all else to do in the Maldives except snorkel. It takes ten and a half hours to fly there from Western Europe. Ten and a half hours! Imagine going all that way to spend it under water.

The Maldives is the kind of holiday destination people talk about specifically to make other people (except those who can't swim) jealous about not going.

'Oh, the snorkelling was marvellous and the sea was so clear.'

What else did you do?

'Oh, you know, chilled out on the beach. Read some trashy novels.'

Sounds pretty much like any other beach holiday to me – apart from the underwater bit, and what's so fantastic about that? Apparently there's a really rare slug/eel thing called a Honeycomb Moray; you can only see it in the Maldives and its body is covered entirely in mucus. Wow. And there's coral – basically, some underwater plants – and a few brightly coloured fish, most of which you can see on *Finding Nemo* or in a rich friend's fish tank. So far, so what?

No doubt there are excellent facilities for golf and water

sports. 'Golf and water sports' – the most depressing double act since Dick and Dom. It's always amusing to see how boring but fantastically expensive beach holidays are livened up in the brochures by reference to other equally tedious activities like golf, sailing, windsurfing and one that really caught my eye, kneeboarding. These are the sort of resorts people go to who own their own wetsuits, 'except you don't really need them because the water's so warm'. It ought to be for that money.

Actually, most people deep down realise that places like the Maldives are dull as ditchwater, so they invent even more ridiculous variations on the theme of 'kneeboarding' to bring an element of danger into the proceedings. So you get kite surfing, paragliding, parasailing, parascending, jetski-windsocking, windkite-jetskiing and jetskiing.

Ah yes, the Jet Ski – the motorised waterborne coffin. As expensive a way to dice with death as a quad bike. Bomb along at thirty miles an hour until you hit a bumpy wave and dislocate both elbows as you somersault over the handlebars, or drift helplessly into the path of another Jet Ski driven by a boozed-up trustafarian toe-rag, and after the collision takes the top of your head off, you can drift downward to become the special lunchtime treat for the mucus-covered Honeycomb Moray eel/slug thing.

# Visit the Pyramids

In Jack Nicholson's rubbish film *The Bucket List* two old guys with time running out try to cram as many big experiences as possible into their last months on earth. Of course, the pyramids are on this list; they're on everybody's list. They are one of the few remaining original seven wonders of the world, but also, as it happens, one of the top ten most disappointing sites in the world, according to British travellers. I'm not quite sure how to process that information, because I hate lists like that.

Naturally, I haven't been – it's too far away and too hot and too expensive and too dangerous (see below) but I'm told one of the really disappointing things is that the pyramids are right next to the unsightly urban sprawl of Cairo. It's like turning off the Birmingham ring road and finding the Hanging Gardens of Babylon. So all those lovely pictures we've seen of the three great pyramids set against the swirling desert sands don't tell the whole story. And if you're actually there it won't look as good – you'll never have an unspoiled view, as I am sure you know by now.

That's the brilliant thing about photography: it allows you to see things in an idealised form; it's why ad men spend fortunes on photographers who can make drab salad cream look amazing by spraying water droplets on the adjacent tomato and using shaving foam instead of Hellmann's

Photography also means you get to see somewhere without having to visit. Imagine how different the world would have been if they'd had photographs in Roman times. I'll bet the Empire would have been a heck of a lot smaller if they'd had sight of some of its furthest outposts *before* they got there.

'What news from Bithynia, Bibulus Scrophulus?'

'I have some photographs here, Caesar.'

'Let's have a look . . . Hmm, it looks like a shit-hole.'

'True, mighty Caesar, but you should see the Old Town, it's really pretty. I have some other pictures here, look; the sunsets are, like, truly amazing. I suggest we raise several legions and conquer the entire territory for the glory of Rome.'

'Yes, well you said that about Britain, didn't you, and look where that got us? Tell you what, this time let's not bother.'

If you're determined to see the pyramids in the flesh, as it were, you should also know that their surface isn't smooth at all; very uneven, in fact, like the face of a particularly pustulant teenager. All the gleaming white limestone that once covered the pyramids and gave them their sharp, clean lines was nicked over the years to build other stuff. What's left looks like the kind of lumpy rubble heap you'd make out of Lego when you were a child. That's the trouble with the Ancient World – no sense of history. Look at the Parthenon in Athens, once the Greek equivalent of St Paul's Cathedral; close up it now looks like the badly maintained former ammunitions dump that it is. I won't bang on about this because I'm doing the Parthenon later, but the observation applies to both monuments – you'll never be disappointed by a nice postcard taken by a professional photographer of the best view from the best angle in the best light at the right time of day to avoid any people.

Another thing to bear in mind about the pyramids (and Egypt in general) is the unmentionable 500lb camel in the room – Islamic terrorism. On top of the heat, the distance, the expense and the sense of anticlimax, if you throw in the threat of being stabbed, shot, beheaded or blown up in the name of Allah, you've got the perfect ingredients for a holiday I'm not going on. Sixty tourists were murdered in the last little local difficulty and since Egypt is the birthplace of Bin Laden's right-hand man and spiritual mentor, Ayman al-Zawahiri, I'd say the chances of it happening again are greater than in somewhere like Ludlow or Newquay or Wells Nex' the Sea.

I'll leave the last word on the pyramids to someone who could write much better than do I, William Thackeray, who saw them in 1844. Even in Victorian times there was a sense that these monuments weren't all they were cracked up to be.

*'The truth is that nobody was seriously moved. And why should they be, because of an exaggeration of bricks ever so enormous? I confess, for my part, that the Pyramids are very big.'*

# Go to Sienna for the Palio

The Palio is a centuries-old horse race around the main square of Sienna in the heart of Tuscany, which is a beautiful place, with wonderfully picturesque towns and villages set in rolling countryside. In fact, it's one of the most delightful spots in Britain or, at least, that's what it feels like. It's not an original observation to note that Tuscany is full of Panama-hatted twerps from Hampstead, but it's enough to make you think twice about going.

On the whole, Italy is one of the places I'd say is worth travelling to, in that it's not too far, not too expensive, not too hot (if you avoid July and August) and crucially the joy of visiting Italy is in the being there, not the doing of anything in particular; drinking wine, eating olives, hanging around and, like Robert De Niro in the song, talking Italian. The thrill-seekers and once-in-a-lifetime holidaymakers tend to steer clear of Italy, although the Palio is something that might tempt them. And maybe that's what's wrong with it: it's too much of an 'event'. The Palio is on twice a year and if you ever tell a seasoned visitor to Chiantishire that you've been to Sienna and missed it they'll look at you as if your testicles were hanging outside your trousers. 'Oh my goodness, how can you go to Sienna and *not* go to the Palio?' – it's spoken in the same tones and by the same people who would be mystified by anyone who'd never been to Glyndebourne; the sort of people who still think there's a 'Season' in London.

Well I went to Sienna once, a long time ago, and I did miss the Palio. When I booked the trip I wasn't really bothered what was going on; whether it was cruel to charge horses at dangerously high speed around a cobbled piazza, I didn't care. I was arranging my honeymoon, in a secluded farmhouse a few miles outside the city. By the time it was all booked, she'd called off the wedding but I was so determined not to waste my money I went anyway. The trouble was she was equally determined to go. Her sister had refused to buy my half of the holiday from me, so we both went, dumper and dumpee together. Look, it was 350 quid each, OK? I have a handy tip for travellers – don't spend a week in a secluded farmhouse with an ex-fiancée, one bedroom and a twenty-foot garden if you want a relaxing break. A day out to Sienna, just after the Palio of course, was an attempt to patch things up a bit, but there was a palpable sense of a great party missed; it was drizzling in that Mediterranean way which is surprisingly Mancunian, and the narrow streets – just wide enough for a Cinquecento – were all displaying one-way signs, designed (for the foreigners who obey them) to direct you all the way around the edge of the city and then off again without ever finding the heart of it – a suitable metaphor in a cheap novel, but maybe this explains a lot of my attitude to 'unmissable, once in a lifetime' events.

# Backpack around Australia

● ● ● ● ● ● ● ● ● ● ● ● ● ● ● ● ● ● ● ● ● ● ● ● ● ● ● ● ● ● ● ● ● ● ● ● ● ●

So many travellers are now boring us with the wonders of Australia that it's become a bit like going to Benidorm, except with more time to get drunk on the way. An amazing 25,000 British tourists go there every year and, unlike the good old days of transportation, most of them come back. But not all. In fact, 2,433 tourists, including 25 children, have died in Australia over the last seven years and despite the fact that I've made up a lot of the statistics in this book, this one is true. Drowning, car crashes and heatstroke are among the big killers, and that's just for starters.

Supposing you survive getting into a car, having a swim or just walking about in the sun; Australia has plenty of other more grisly ways for you to die. There are killer crocodiles lurking in a few centimetres of water that you have no hope of seeing until it's too late; sharks that snack at most of the popular beaches; deadly poisonous jellyfish that can kill with one touch; hideous, poisonous toads which can make you throw up just by looking at them; to say nothing of the three million varieties of deadly poisonous spider, including that one that hides under toilet seats waiting to sink its fangs into your backside.

Even Australia's cuddly national symbols have a violent streak – but don't take my word for it, this is what Ranger Craig Adams of the Australian Wildlife Park has to say: 'People don't realise a koala will give you a nasty bite or carve you up with its claws,' he said. 'A wombat can knock you over.' And you'd think yourself lucky to meet a mere wombat if you were the thirteen-year-old boy who, a few years ago, was viciously beaten up by a kangaroo on a golf course.

This kind of wild behaviour perhaps explains the Australians' ambivalent attitude towards their best-known marsupials – on the one hand the kangaroo is the Aussie national symbol, and on the other hand Australians make handbags out of their scrotums and bottle openers out of their little front feet.

And if you're still not put off, just think about the people who actually live in Australia; the people who *choose* to live there, their minds numbed by endless repeats of *The Bill* and *Heartbeat*. Maybe that's why Australia is a happy hunting ground for British comics: it's a whole new audience for old material. Even Billy Connolly still gets work down there.

The Australian music charts are another great cultural barometer – songs by and about cricketers are big news and one of the biggest hits of recent years was a tribute to the sport's greatest ever spin bowler: 'Warney, Put Your Wanger Away!' And this is what happens in places where they have running water and electricity. If you should actually leave the big-city sophistication of, say, Perth, to get closer to the 'real' Australia, you'll find an unsavoury mix of backpacker murderers, baby-eating dingoes, casual racism and extreme facial hair. Is all this worth it just to come back with a photo of a big red rock?

# Run with the Bulls in Pamplona

If you've ever seen the film *City Slickers* with Billy Crystal, you know exactly the kind of people who want to do this: tragic, middle-aged blokes, like the one played by Billy Crystal, whose lives are so comfortable that they have to risk crippling injury to remind themselves that they are still alive.

If you haven't seen *City Slickers*, it's about three friends who . . . well, that's not really important, but it opens on the San Fermin festival in a northern Spanish town called Pamplona.

Whatever the true story of Saint Fermin might be, he certainly wasn't dragged to his death by bulls in Pamplona because he died in France, but any old excuse to bolt a cattle market onto a religious festival and make a few pesetas. The whole thing is now caught up with bullfighting and the general humiliation of the animals, until a bloke with a funny hat and a cloak sticks a spear into them. It's the kind of tourist attraction which says, 'Why not join us in our national pastime of animal torture? Now that throwing donkeys out of bell-towers has been outlawed, it's the next best thing.'

According to my trusty sources at Wikipedia, what happens is that the streets of Pamplona become jammed with tourists and then the authorities release hundreds of jittery bulls into the narrow alleyways, presumably in the hope they will trample to death a few tardy South Africans. Actually, as a macho pastime it's not even that impressive – everyone is told they have no chance of outrunning the animals, so all they have to do is run along for a hundred yards or so before jumping out of the way over a small fence. You can probably get the same adrenaline rush by playing chicken on your local ring road.

Some hopelessly idealistic people at PETA, the animal-rights group, have organised the 'Running of the Nudes' as a rival attraction to the bull thing. It's true. What happens is, a lot of very attractive models run around the town with no clothes on, in the hope that all the drunken men who come to Pamplona will prefer to run around after them, rather than join in the bull run. What the lovely ladies of PETA have failed to realise is that most blokes will simply do both, so as a distraction I think it will backfire and it actually makes it quite difficult for me to advise men not to go.

# Read Kafka in Prague

· · · · · · · · · · · · · · · · · · · · · · · · · · · · · · · · · · · · ·

This is a must for any pretentious, avant-garde and, quite literally, Bohemian student-type – usually a man and definitely the sort who pays far too much attention to his shoes and trousers. It's the bibliophile's equivalent of 'keeping it real' and implies that absorbing an author's work in the incorrect setting equates to reading a large-print version or one with the long words edited out.

It also assumes you have a phenomenal amount of time on your hands, because presumably this pretentious ambition doesn't apply solely to Kafka. Are you also obliged to go to equal lengths in pursuit of other authors' feelings for their subject matter? Like sailing up the Congo to read *Heart of Darkness*, snooping around the suburbs of Los Angeles with Raymond Chandler or grinding through Ben Elton's works in a highly efficient sausage factory?

And what about science fiction? Where is the correct place to read HG Wells? In the future? OK, Prague is easier to get to than the future, but if you've been to Prague recently you'll know that no one goes there to read a book, unless it's *101 Top Stag Weekend Destinations To Throw Up In Before You Die.*

Once upon a time in communist Prague you could go to the opera for 50p or enjoy authentic Czech shadow puppetry for free. But now you are obliged to saturate yourself with Pilsner Urquell, charge around Wenceslas Square with a dozen other braying thirty-year-olds and vomit over the side of the Charles Bridge – making it difficult to fully appreciate the sense of isolation that *The Castle* creates.

If you must share Kafka's feelings of hopelessness, alienation, persecution and futility, don't bother going to Prague – go to work in an insurance brokers like he did; spend five years studying law, contract tuberculosis or clinical depression, a migraine, insomnia, constipation and boils.

Or, failing that, try buying some batteries in Argos.

# Visit the Grand Canyon

● ● ● ● ● ● ● ● ● ● ● ● ● ● ● ● ● ● ● ● ● ● ● ● ● ● ● ● ● ● ● ● ● ●

How could I possibly have a problem with this, you may ask? It has to be one of the true wonders of the world, a massive ten-mile-wide gash in the earth and a drop of 5,000 feet. It is one of the most spectacular views you can experience anywhere and from a purely geological point of view it's a glimpse into a zillion years of Earth's history. Yes, that's all very well, but – if you've been paying attention, you surely know what's coming now – the practicalities of enjoying that view are monumentally tedious.

If you want to travel from one side to the other, from the South Rim to the North Rim – about ten miles as the crow flies – it will take you five hours. Why would anyone want to do that? Well, the South Rim is the bit where everyone goes because it's easier to get to, so it's completely mobbed, the traffic is horrendous and the crowds are twelve deep. So if you want a bit of peace and quiet in which to soak up this awesome experience, add five hours to your flight time of ten hours from London to Phoenix plus a 3½-hour drive from Phoenix to the South Rim. Of course you could always visit the Grand Canyon in winter – November to February is the least crowded time, and how bad can the weather be along the Colorado River at that time of year? Well apparently, winter storms can frequently and completely wipe out the view you've travelled 5,000 miles to see and there are no entrance-fee refunds if this happens, so the answer to 'how bad can the weather get?' is, 'bad enough for me'. And there's no guarantee, if you do visit the Canyon out of season, that you'll have the place to yourself; you may have to share your holiday with some very intimidating wildlife. Because September to October is the rutting season for elk, moose and caribou, and you might just find yourself on the receiving end of a charge by 1,000lb of sexually aroused ungulate.

Come on . . . isn't it tempting just to click on the Grand Canyon official website and view the whole thing online in the comfort of your own home? Just imagine the lack of tension, travel fatigue and high expenditure as you sample the amazing computerised virtual tour from an imaginary helicopter. Or if you fancy a bit more excitement (I'm not a complete killjoy!) go to the Science Museum in London, pay two quid and you can sit in a mini-helicopter simulator which will fly you over the Grand Canyon and shake you about a bit into the bargain.

There *is* something in the idea of the Grand Canyon that does appeal to me – the drop, the sheer height of it and that feeling you get in the backs of your legs when you look down from a precipice. I'm a total fraidy cat in the face of imminent death or severe injury, but there is something about heights that is tremendously exciting. I imagine, though, that the really vertiginous bits of the Grand Canyon are surrounded by viewing platforms and railings and, although you can trek down to the very bottom of the great crack to the river, in the pictures I've seen it all seems to spread out as you descend and loses its loftiness. I could be completely wrong, of course. And then again, maybe I've been confusing the actual Grand Canyon with wherever it is that the Roadrunner lives in those Warner Brothers cartoons. You know, when Wile E Coyote falls off a cliff or his Acme Rocket Bike sends him a thousand feet into the air, only to plummet to earth and gradually disappear into a tiny dot and a puff of smoke? If the Grand Canyon is like that, count me in. I'd consider a ten-hour flight and 3½-hour car journey as nought if, at the other end of it, I could see a roadrunner being chased at high speed by a coyote with a knife and fork, as an ACME van speeds by, delivering a huge cannon or a jar of earthquake pills.

But I reckon it's not like that. For starters, I know that the real roadrunner is a dull, unexceptional little bird, which doesn't go Beep-Beep. And a real coyote is a sort of ugly, scruffy dog which doesn't have a knife and fork, never wears a crash helmet and is completely incapable of tying an anvil on to a coiled spring. Perhaps this is a metaphor for the Grand Canyon itself, and maybe the whole concept of 'once in a lifetime' holidays. The reality is never what you hope it will be. So don't risk it, my friends; it just might be boring.

# Go to Buenos Aires to see Boca Juniors vs River Plate

This local football derby in Argentina was declared by the *Observer* to be the top 'sporting thing you must do before you die'. If you have paid only scant attention to the other entries in this book, you'll know that a talking dog performing brain surgery wouldn't tempt me to travel 10,000 miles, let alone a football match, and least of all one in which the outcome is of no interest to anybody. And before you start factoring in aeroplane tickets to South America and taxis from airports, you have to remember that going through the turnstile of virtually any football match anywhere is outrageously poor value for what you're actually getting in return. In fact, if you wanted to find a definition of an overrated activity – which, since you're reading a whole book about the subject, you probably do – then football is it. And if I hear one more person call it 'The Beautiful Game', I'll throw up. Come on – what's beautiful about it? It began in the Middle Ages as an extended fight over a pig's bladder between villages and not much has changed since.

Yes, a good football match can be exciting; it can put you through the emotional wringer like nothing else can if you have a particular fondness for one team. But it only properly rewards you if all the others fail. In fact, if Manchester United don't win a trophy all season then all's well with the world. Not only does this not happen very often, but in no way could this be described as a 'beautiful' sentiment. You'll search in vain, too, for any beauty in the way the game is structured and funded; the shady businessmen who bankroll the big clubs are now foreign rather than local and the cash comes from labyrinthine fiscal jiggery-pokery rather than the scrap yards, chains of butcher's shops and used car-dealerships of old.

Then there's the gravy train that follows the game – the agents, the sponsorships, the TV deals that schedule games for any reason other than the convenience of the supporters. They bombard us with endless hyperbole about how the Premier League is the best in the world and see nothing wrong in a season featuring 27 massive must-win Grand Slam Super

Sunday Arsenal/Man U/Liverpool/Chelsea games. You can thank Sky TV for all that, and the endless shots of managers on the touchline twirling like dervishes and choking on their chewing gum, and hordes of fat Geordies blubbing like babies in their replica shirts as Newcastle United flop again.

I blame Pelé. He's responsible for the 'beautiful game' quote. His 1970 Brazil team may have played fancier football than most, but there were enough dirty tricks and skulduggery in the Mexico '70 tournament to cheapen the world champions' achievements. In South America, the corruption and violence in football is truly world class. Andres Escobar, the unfortunate scorer of the own goal that put Columbia out of the '94 World Cup, was murdered on his return home. In Argentina, the *barras bravas* or hooligans are far more ambitious than any we have in Britain. They blackmail players, managers and chairmen with threats of violence and visits to their houses; the police have been known to *pay* them not to cause trouble at certain matches.

But it's the noise and the passion and the threat of violence that make the Boca Juniors/River Plate derby so 'attractive'. All the travel blogs and football fan sites on the Internet attest to the tremendous atmosphere of intimidation and hatred – 'way better than the Old Firm derby'. Yes, hats off to the Argies, they certainly put 400 years of Scottish religious bigotry in the shade. Since everyone's Catholic in Argentina they've opted for the simple Rich vs Poor battle lines instead, and they can boast a death toll of 74 fans on a single day in 1968. The beautiful game, eh? All the skill in the world can be obliterated by a single image of a bare-chested young idiot with his arms outstretched, beckoning a huge crowd of opposing hooligans to come and have a go if they think they're hard enough, or however you say that in Spanish.

So rather than participate in the myth of the beautiful game by travelling all the way to Buenos Aires, you could turn on your television set and celebrate an undeniably wondrous thing in modern football – the beautiful mind of Sky Sport's anchorman, Jeff Stelling. I said that Sky have done a lot of damage to British football by pouring their TV millions into the pockets of a few clubs, and so they have. But Jeff embodies what is truly good about the game, and anyone who appreciates the wonder of Jeff can truly understand the grip that football has on people, particularly men. It's all to do with numbers. Jeff's programme on a Saturday afternoon is chock-full of numbers – every inch of the screen is jam-packed with figures and statistics, but there are even more in Jeff's head. As dozens of football results come flooding in, Jeff Stelling can, in the blink of an eye, bring to our attention that Forfar Athletic's left back has scored on his wedding anniversary for the past three seasons running. Facts like this can mesmerise the angriest of football hooligans and if I were in charge of world football (it's a long shot but I'm working on it) I'd have Jeff Stelling piped on to the big screens at every football match on the planet.

# See the Parthenon

Once upon a time this would have been really worth seeing – not just because of what it is, but where it is. To visit Athens in the fifth century BC was to witness the very apex of civilisation; the birthplace of Western democracy, philosophy and literature. You could say Athens was very much like Rome, but without the public murder as a spectator sport. The Romans have always seemed a bit oafish – clever, skilful, muscular and resourceful, yes, but also brutal and crude; the Germans of their day, compared to the smart, sophisticated, cultured, literate 'French' of Athens. The Romans put most ingenious discoveries of science and mathematics to practical use in big engineering projects, whereas the Athenians had the ideas in the first place but couldn't really see the point in doing anything with them – maybe they just couldn't be arsed?

A couple of Athenians called Iktinos and Kallikrates did pull their fingers out when they built the Parthenon. It's undeniably a work of genius, designed so that the outer columns incline together slightly to meet at an imaginary point almost two miles above it, so that from a distance it looks perfectly square. It also has an ever-so-slightly convex stone floor to shed rainwater, and it was decorated with an astonishing carved marble frieze that was legendary in its own time.

Despite all that, it's still not worth going to Athens to see it because the place has been a complete tip for centuries. It would be ironic if the capital city of the country that gave birth to the Olympics should be rejuvenated by money generated by the modern Olympics staged there in 2004. Well, it would be if it were true, but it isn't. In fact, the money went on a new underground system, a facelift for the airport and some grand stadiums, which are still fenced off and patrolled by dog-handlers so ordinary Athenians can't use them.

No one is expecting the Athenians to restore the Parthenon to its former glory; the image of the Parthenon everyone has is of a damaged masterpiece. But it's not damaged in a good way like the Colosseum in Rome, which is somehow enhanced by the cutaway sections showing you how it functioned. You can't really blame the Greeks for the broken bits – the Parthenon was brutally damaged by a Venetian attack on an Ottoman stronghold in the Turko-Venetian war of 1684 (Turks vs Venetians – who knew?). The Turks were using it to store gunpowder so it's fair to say they didn't have the building's best interests at heart. Fortunately for civilisation, Lord Elgin looted the world-famous frieze and stuck it in the British Museum for a hundred years, and you have to argue we did a better job of looking after it than the Greeks would have.

Although a major tarting-up operation is now underway, to see the Parthenon in its current state is a reminder that, from the summit of civilisation, Athens has fallen a heck of a way, so I would advise anyone who wants to immerse themselves in the glories of Ancient Greece to get *Jason and the Argonauts* out on DVD.

# Go On a Balloon Safari

• • • • • • • • • • • • • • • • • • • • • • • • • • • • • • • • • •

Like the barge, the car ferry, the 2CV and the bicycle, I love the idea of a hot-air balloon because it's slow and unhurried and graceful. But combine it with a safari and all the magic is ruined. Like 'Swimming with Dolphins', going on safari involves travelling quite a long way and spending quite a lot of money to see what you can see in England – zoos and safari parks have loads of lions and zebras and the occasional elephant. London Zoo has even got giraffes! It is quite pricey to get in – over fifteen quid for grown-ups – but if you stay all day it's less than two quid an hour; not bad. Going on a balloon safari in Africa is way more expensive – it's £250 just to get in the balloon and you have to get up at the crack of dawn to get the air currents or something. I know you have to do that for balloon flights in Britain but I'd rather get up at the crack of dawn in my own bed, thanks. Then there's the prospect of trying to spot wild animals, peering through binoculars and forcing yourself to get excited because you've glimpsed a couple of ears poking through a bush. David Attenborough has spent a lifetime following these creatures around, and some of his cameramen have sat still for so long waiting for a decent shot they have been known to fuse with the landscape; we really don't need to do it.

I haven't mentioned the risks yet. Suppose you do see some wild animals; some lions, for instance. What if the balloon happens to crash? It's quite possible. You're going to have to be able to run at 30mph if you want to avoid being jumped on and bitten in half by a 300lb lioness. The big daddy lion doesn't do much catching himself; he strolls up later to rip off the best bits of you. Just as a matter of interest, the worst outbreak of man-eating lion attacks was in Tanzania in the 1930s when 1,500 people were taken and eaten by a single pride of lions. I don't know if they'd been on a balloon safari, but you never know.

# Bungee Jump

Best loved by competitive stag party crackpots, the bungee jump is one of several near-death experiences young men have devised to replace the thrill of being shot or blown up in a war.

You either climb up to a high bridge or get hoisted to the top of a crane, trusting with your life some beardy you've never met before, as he ties a length of elastic to your feet, and then you jump off, hoping the bungee isn't too long or else your head will smash into whatever lies beneath.

Of course, that may not happen, the bungee may just come loose because it wasn't tied on properly; as you hurtle downwards like Wile E Coyote from a *Roadrunner* cartoon, you wonder whether it was worth it for a few seconds of adrenaline rush.

Some of the listed injuries on offer to bungee jumpers (apart from severe cranial trauma) include rope burn, dislocations, eye trauma and uterine prolapse – nice to have a special little something for the ladies. I came across one particularly unpleasant clip on the Internet of a Dutch man whose jump was technically perfect apart from the fact he was so scared he upside-down shat himself.

It's all a far cry from the origins of bungee jumping . . . er, actually no, it isn't a far cry at all. The Pacific islands of Vanuatu have a rite of passage for young men in which they leap from a huge tower with a springy creeper tied to their ankle. The length of the creeper is calculated to be just sufficient to allow the young man's head to brush the ground before it bounces him back up again. His only reward is that before his jump he is permitted to be as rude as he likes to anyone in his village.

Everyone says Vanuatu is the happiest place in the world; perhaps bungee jumping has something to do with that? Maybe, but in Vanuatu they also worship Prince Philip as a god and the national currency is pigs' tusks. Should we try that too?

Maybe it was the 'wacky' culture surrounding bungee jumping that appealed so much to those 'completely mad' toffs from Oxford University's Dangerous Sports Club, whose claim to fame is bringing bungee jumping to the world's attention. Thanks for that, guys – bungee jumping can join mortar boards, *Brideshead Revisited*, punting, jumping off Magdalen Bridge on May Day and the Rupert Murdoch Chair of Language and Communication as one of the many reasons that some people are slightly embarrassed to admit they attended what is otherwise quite a respectable university.

# Eat Fugu Fish in Japan

Those who ruin their lives with a constant quest for new experiences divide into several camps, but one of the most contemptible is the gastronomic adventurer. Gastronomic ambition has moved beyond things like caviar, lobster, champagne and foie gras. Since most of these are now available in Tesco, adventurous epicureans are having to resort to much more extreme edible experiences. You can go on a quest for intensity of flavour – the appliest apple, beefiest beef, the snailiest snail porridge – the Heston Blumenthal way, for those who like their food prepared by Dr No using test tubes and syringes.

Or you can head off in pursuit of well-nigh illegal delicacies. Tiger is on the menu in China and there are, no doubt, places in the world where you can eat elephant, dolphin, fruit-bat and marmoset – for the pervert-gourmand, the more endangered the better. And if the food endangers *you*, then you're really cooking on gas. Why not join the testy young men who like to gamble with a late-night kebab from a corner shop or street van, or line up for a bucket of Fried Chicken? If the food doesn't get you, the fight in the queue will.

With fugu fish you get danger plus exotic. If you think you've never seen one, it's in *Finding Nemo*; the one with the spikes that inflates itself when it's angry or frightened. The poison in the fugu fish (tetrodotoxin) is one of the deadliest known to man; it's a thousand times stronger than cyanide and there is no known antidote.

There's absolutely no reason to eat fugu; it doesn't even taste very nice – quite bland, apparently (you could say it has a nutty flavour if you want to sound like you know about food –all chefs do this, 'mmm, this asparagus has a wonderful nutty taste'). No, fugu's popularity is due to the fact it might kill you. The liver and the ovaries are the really poisonous bits but the skin also packs a punch – you have to be a specially licensed and trained chef to serve it. The license was introduced in 1958 but that didn't stop 178 people dropping dead from fugu poisoning that year. Some hard-core nutters catch it and eat it themselves, deliberately seeking out the liver for the actual poisoning experience (is this like paying extra for sex without a condom, I wonder?), which at its best involves a numbing of the lips and tongue. Frankly, I can get this from my dentist for about thirty quid, with free x-rays thrown in, or I could catch Bell's palsy and get extensive facial nerve damage for nothing.

As a fugu eater, you'll be lucky if tingling lips are all you experience after you've tucked in. If you're unlucky, you will be paralysed within minutes and unable to breathe but – here's the bonus – fully conscious as you asphyxiate. Some people paralysed by fugu have been thought to be dead only to recover hours before cremation. (Cremation – there's an experience to try before you die!) Actually, perhaps this would be a fitting way to go for all those thrill seekers and adrenaline junkies . . . yes, on second thoughts, go ahead and eat some fugu fish in Japan. Go on, tuck in.

# **Drink a Yard of Ale**

• • • • • • • • • • • • • • • • • • • • • • • • • • • • • • • • •

This is listed on quite a few websites along with other examples of extreme consumption like 'Eat a chilli pepper', 'Go to an Indian restaurant and order the hottest thing on the menu', 'Try absinthe' and 'Swallow the worm from a tequila bottle'.

I actually own a yard of ale. It was hidden in the attic of a house I moved into. It's an amazing thing – an elongated trumpet of glass with a round end, capable of holding up to three pints of liquid. It takes skill to make a yard of ale, and a lot of practice to drink one. The glass bulb lets air in and propels liquid out, so once you've tipped it halfway, a pint and a half of beer will shoot down your throat, or your neck. Manipulating the glass and holding down the booze without vomiting has become a real rite of passage for rugby-loving tosspots the world over, but particularly in Australia, where one rugby-loving tosspot called Bob Hawke set the world record for downing a yard of ale and then, naturally, became prime minister.

But pity the poor glassblower of yesteryear, spending hours over a hot . . . er . . . thing that you blow glass over, carefully blowing it into an elongated trumpet shape and rounding the end into a perfect sphere – just so that fart-lighting, hairy-arsed rugger-buggers would have something to do on those rare nights out when they aren't dressing up as women.

It wasn't meant to be this way. The yard of ale was actually invented as a way of handing a decent-sized quantity of beer to a thirsty, dusty coachman without him having to get down from his seat. The air in the glass bulb mechanism propelled the beer down the glass so the coachman didn't have to tip it very far; it wasn't meant to be full to the brim. No one wanted a pissed-up coachman shaking his passengers around the nation's highways or inflicting blowback vomit on them through the coach window.

I like beer. But 'downing it in one' is something I have never understood. It's usually accompanied by random shouting and banging on the table and followed ultimately by some kind of scatological humiliation of the downer. Tragic Ulrika Jonsson, the TV tart with the heart, famously could down a pint of lager in one. I'm not sure what else she could do, apart from reading the weather. That must have been a tough career choice for her – 'should I focus on the weather-reading or the lager-drinking?' In the end Vic and Bob persuaded her to make a sketch show based quite heavily on downing a pint of lager in one. It's hard to say if it's done her any damage but it certainly hasn't sharpened her sense of who'd make a good husband.

There is a place where beer drinking is absolutely embedded in the national culture but hasn't created a strain of offensively loud, violent, oafishly incontinent gits like the British or the Australians. Coincidentally, they also revere the beer glass with the curiously shaped bottom. The place is Belgium – try finding that on a list of places you must go before you die. Belgium is brilliant. First of all it's not far away, it's easy to get to and pretty cheap. The place is full of eccentric geniuses with a tradition of great art, wonderful food and fantastic places to drink. They also produce about three million different beers of top quality, all of them with their own glass. The best and most eccentric of these is Kwak. What a brilliant name for a beer! Kwak. The correct way to drink Kwak is out of the special Kwak glass, specially designed for the drinking of Kwak (I do love that word). As it is round-bottomed, you have to rest the glass in a purpose-built wooden stand, a bit like something out of the school chemistry lab. Bosteels Brewers, who make Kwak, claim that, like the yard of ale, it was designed to give to coachmen, who would clip it on to their coach seat in a special niche. I prefer to think that the Bosteel family, being Belgian, just thought it looked nice.

# Go White-Water Rafting

• • • • • • • • • • • • • • • • • • • • • • • • • • • • • • • • • • • •

Apart from the sheer thrill of almost smashing your brains out on the rocks in a fast-flowing river, white-water rafting is supposed to be great for team bonding – a favourite corporate away-day/weekend activity for city bankers, admen and home-grown terrorist organisations: the 7/7 bombers did a lot of their best blue-sky thinking on a white-water rafting weekend in Wales.

The top destination for such holidays is the Colorado River – not the Grand Canyon bit, but a lot higher up where it's more dangerous. For me, a group of mates paddling down a fast-flowing river in a boat throws up one word – *Deliverance*. I think you know what's coming. You will be laughing away like a teenager on a roller coaster for a few hundred yards until it starts to get really bumpy, then the boat will capsize; you will all be thrown out and one of your party will suffer one of those horrific bone-sticking-out-through-the-flesh fractures. It'll probably be the one who looks most like Burt Reynolds, and while he screams in agony, a couple of you will wander off looking for help – only to be captured by some cross-eyed mountain men, who will tell you that you sure got a purty mouth.

You will then be royally buggered while squealing like a pig. Fortunately one of your other mates will kill one of the mountain men with a bow and arrow. After that, you'll all have to bury the body because the local inbreds will never give you a fair trial and *you will live with the guilt for the rest of your lives.* You might scoff, but this scenario happens more often than you think – in fact, last year four out of every five river-based adventure holidays ended with serious injury, male rape and revenge killing – I'm sure I read that somewhere.

# Skydive

• • • • • • • • • • • • • • • • • • • • • • • • • • • • • • • • • •

Jumping out of a plane for fun must seem so strange to those people who were forced to do it in a real combat situation and would never ever do it again for all the money in the world. Why stop at modern warfare in your search for thrills? Why not try charging across a muddy field while hundreds of stout yeomen fire longbows at you? Often such acts of recklessness and stupidity are excused in the name of charity. But why should I sponsor someone simply because they are putting their life at risk, however noble the cause? 'I'm going to head-butt a chainsaw for Motor Neurone Disease, can I put you down for fifty quid?'

Some people do one parachute jump for charity but then get seriously addicted to skydiving. One friend of mine was completely hooked until one day his chute didn't open properly – after about twenty seconds of plummeting, he blacked out and came to in a tree. You know those dreams you have when you are falling and wake up with a jolt just before you hit the ground? He has those every night, only they're not dreams, they're memory.

Seasoned skydivers, even my mate who has since, unbeliev-ably, taken up jumping again, say the adrenaline rush when you jump out of the plane is worth all the training and the preparation time and the fear. No, no, no, no, no! How can it possibly be worth it? I don't think queuing for half an hour at a theme park for the Big Dipper or Thunder Mountain or Vomit Passage or whatever it's called is worth it, never mind leaping into space at 13,000 feet with only a square of silk keeping you airborne. There are about a million reasons not to skydive. I won't list them all here, but the main ones are: I don't want to pay 200 quid to be trained for three weeks in basic technique, having someone push me off a ten-foot wall to simulate landing; I don't want to feel my bowels turn to hot-and-sour soup in a rickety plane and then jump out of it. I don't want to smash into the ground at 124 miles an hour and have my leg bones driven up under my armpits or land face first and have my eyeballs pop out through the back of my skull, or, assuming the chute does open, float helplessly into the propeller blades of a plane on the ground and be turned into a human smoothie. For a full list of all the other reasons, you can buy a copy of my next book – *1,000,000 Reasons Not To Skydive.*

# Drive at 100mph

• • • • • • • • • • • • • • • • • • • • • • • • • • • • • • • •

Not that much of a tall order nowadays, as this can quite easily be achieved through sheer carelessness. Modern cars can touch a hundred at the involuntary twitch of a right knee.

But 'tonning up' used to be something to brag about, like losing your virginity. The needle nudging up to 100 used to be so scary it made you wobble your steering wheel in disbelief. These days 130 is probably the target; that, I think, is progress for you.

It was different in Aldous Huxley's day: travelling in a car at 60mph had such an inebriating effect on him that he declared speed 'a new type of drug . . . an efficient and less harmful substitute for alcohol and cocaine'. Ah, Aldous, you poor fool, on this as on so many things: totally wrong. Never mind the 'less harmful' bit, nothing is ever a substitute for alcohol. It just joins it in the mix, as the hundreds of thousands of people, whose lives have been ruined by drunk drivers since Huxley wrote those words, will testify.

However, it is true there is something intoxicating about a minor infringement of the law, like breaking a speed limit, which makes you feel outrageous for a moment. There's a wonderful scene in the shit-but-still-watchable Roger Moore film, *The Man Who Haunted Himself*. Roger, an uptight city gent, is on his regular

30mph drive home to Weybridge when he gets a funny look in his eye. The famous eyebrow goes up and the foot goes down. Soon, Rog is doing seventy and appears to be morphing into a different person, and the eyebrow keeps ascending as he accelerates until he smashes his Rover 3-litre into some road-works. The car disintegrates, his soul divides in two and another version of himself, more wild and daring and exciting than his old one, usurps his job, wife, house and family. Come on, it could happen. Somewhere out there could be another version of Richard Hammond who says to Jeremy Clarkson, 'piss off, it's your turn to drive the rocket'.

With today's cars, as any incarnation of Richard Hammond will tell you, how *fast* they go is not the issue, it's how resistant they are to flipping over and breaking up, like Roger Moore's 3-litre. But what is so appealing to humans about speed? Why is it like a drug? Why are we programmed to want to go faster?

I suppose it must have been good news for the turnip delivery man in, say, 1930 when he discovered he could get his turnips from Grantham to King's Lynn in less than a week, thanks to his new-fangled motor van. But when sugar-beet man overtook turnip man in his brand new Root Vegetable Van mark II, the envy kicked in.

The problem with speed is that, technology being as it is, someone will always go faster than you. It's a metaphor for the whole of this book. What motivates people to cram their lives full of ever more amazing experiences is their all-consuming desire to have a richer life than anyone else they know. But the law of progress means there will always be a quicker way of doing something around the next corner. Look at one of the greatest labour-saving devices ever – the lift, or elevator, if this book should turn up in an American remainder bin.

Imagine a box you can walk into that will lift you hundreds of feet in the air to save you walking up some stairs! Even with such time-saving devices as lifts people still cannot bear to wait an extra second. Otis Elevators employ dedicated experts in the field of time delays and waiting experiences – they have discovered that even a three-second 'door dwell' (delay between pressing the door-close button and the doors actually closing) can be too much for some. There is so much unnecessary pressing of the door-close button in Japan and South Korea that building managers have, unbeknownst to the passengers, disabled the door-close function, so its users are pressing it for nothing. They leave the redundant button in place because pressing it makes people feel better.

I used to own a Citroen 2CV – a masterpiece of French design. Its size and shape was dictated by the brief to transport a hat-wearing farmer together with his wife and a tray of eggs across a ploughed field. Suffice to say I loved everything about it, especially when heavy motorway traffic allowed me to trundle past various high-performance cars stuck in the outside lane. Very few things have given me greater pleasure than the look on the Porsche driver's face as I crawled by his window.

Unfortunately there must have been another element in the design brief of the 2CV which ensures it rusts through and breaks in half after five years. So now I have a bicycle and, believe me, the effect on other drivers is just the same, if not better than the 2CV. The added beauty being not only can a bike freewheel past slow-moving traffic, it can jump red lights, go the wrong way down one-way streets, cut in front of buses and ride on pavements. Car drivers often rather stupidly ask, why is it that cyclists always jump red lights? The answer is simple: because we can and you can't. Your anger brings us joy.

Fortunately, there is now a 'slow movement' afoot in Europe; it rejects haste and impatience and over-stimulation. It began in Italy and has now established a set of conditions (a bit like those for joining the Euro) that towns and cities must fulfil if they want to join. Appropriately, Ludlow in Shropshire and Diss in Norfolk are already in. Why not lobby for your town to join today?

# Ride a Horse on a Beach

• • • • • • • • • • • • • • • • • • • • • • • • • • • • • • • • • • •

I'll admit that this always looks great in films and those adverts for holidays in Ireland. Assuming you feel comfortable with the idea of being thrown around by half a ton of untrustworthy animal and can actually ride a horse, it may possibly be good fun. But come on, is it really worth the effort?

I've been to a lot of beaches . . . well, OK, not a lot; I don't like beaches particularly, but the ones I have been to have very poor horse access. To get anywhere near these beaches you have to descend about 300 steep steps to the seafront bit where all the slot machines are. Then there are always some Victorian railings and a pretty sheer drop on to the actual beach, where you're faced with 25 yards of really big horse-unfriendly pebbles before you get to the sea. How's Prancer going to negotiate all that without breaking a fetlock?

So you'll probably manage half an hour, max, of trotting and galloping along the water's edge, kicking up quite a bit of spray no doubt, before you get a bit bored. This is going to have to be early in the morning because there'll be all sorts of people in the way otherwise (See 'Sex on a Beach', 'Bonfire on a Beach'). So in order to enjoy the full experience, you'll have to get up at about, what – 6 a.m.? Then have breakfast, go down to the stables, give Prancer his breakfast too, get the saddle and stuff, ride all the way down to the beach, all before you begin to tackle the aforementioned assault course. Maybe you'd have just as much fun riding the horse somewhere normal like a field. Or how's this for an idea: if you like beaches so much, go for a bloody walk.

# Ride a Horse on a Beach Bareback

· · · · · · · · · · · · · · · · · · · · · · · · · · · · · · · · · · ·

Riding bareback is seen, of course, as 'the natural thing to do' and part of a hippy-chick fantasy which involves sitting round a camp fire (on a beach, natch), strumming an out of tune acoustic guitar and singing the very worst of Tracey Chapman.

All over the Internet you can find people evangelising about bareback riding as being a deeper bond between horse and human; more comfortable, easier and even safer than riding with a saddle. They are probably the same people who say that antibiotics are dangerous, that doctors shouldn't go near pregnant women and that genetically modified foods, which can survive diseases and bring nourishment to starving people in the poorest parts of the world, should be banned at all costs because they are simply not 'natural' enough. I presume bareback riders shun the 'unnatural' to the extent that they won't wear riding hats and insist on head-butting the ground as they fall off to strengthen their bond with the earth.

Yes, those horrible saddle designers (whoever they were), created their new-fangled horse seat purely to insult the noble steed and proclaim man's dominance over the animal kingdom. Never mind assembling a comfortable bum cushion with stirrups to keep your feet in the right place and stop you falling off the horse – that must have been of secondary importance.

Professional rodeo riders have described bareback riding as 'like sitting on a pogo stick attached to a jackhammer', but what would they know, the bread-heads? If you add in the requirement to fire a weapon, like a rifle, from the back of a horse, saddles begin to make a lot more sense. American Indians were said to be the most skilful riders on the planet because they rode bareback everywhere from infancy. But the White Man had the saddle and they didn't. And who won? I'm only asking.

# Learn to Ride a Motorbike

• • • • • • • • • • • • • • • • • • • • • • • • • • • • • • • •

No question – riding a motorbike is exciting. The problem is it's only exciting if you do it badly, and then you might well die. Even if you don't, the injuries you could sustain would be a serious hindrance to an easy life. Broken shoulders and pelvises, serious head injuries, road rash – which is a nice way of saying the top layer of your skin gets scraped off – 'bikers arm' (nerve damage causing permanent paralysis), oh, and fractured elbows, knees, wrists, fingers, spine and neck. This just doesn't sit easily with the *Can't Be Arsed* ethos. The potential fun is just not worth the risk.

Steve McQueen in *The Great Escape*, Elvis in *Roustabout* and Jack Nicholson in *Easy Rider* all seemed to be having a whale of a time, but they were the kind of guys who would look death in the face and laugh sardonically; plus they would look stupid in a crash helmet. I wouldn't be at all cocky when staring death in the face – and I'm sure the best a crash helmet can do in an accident is keep your face and skull together temporarily. I imagine when someone takes it off your head would look like Darth Vader's at the end of the *Star Wars* saga – a rather pale egg with a big crack in it.

If you want to approach the motorcycle properly and with respect, you're going to find it a bit boring. Training for a test is really dull. Obviously you have to wear a helmet, which makes it impossible to see where you're going, and follow a man around town for hours, wearing an orange bib while your co-learners buzz around behind in *their* orange bibs, looking over shoulders and pottering round corners at a snail's pace.

And whatever they may teach you, they can't teach other drivers to give a shit about your safety, or look both ways before they pull out and cause you to smash your face through the driver's window. Whether you're Steve McQueen or Captain Cautious, as a motorcycle rider you are thirty times more likely to be scraped off the road than if you were in a car.

Motorcycle instructors say that a lot of these accidents are due to a basic misunderstanding of how a motorcycle works. Apparently, to turn left, you first have to steer right. Which is crazy, isn't it? But no, this is supposed to be an instinctive reaction everyone develops when learning to ride a bicycle as a kid. A slight turn to the right tips the bike over to the left. So if it's instinctive, why tell us about it? You're not supposed to think about instinctive things – it makes you self-conscious and then you get the instinctive thing wrong! So if someone pulls out from the left in front of me, I shouldn't turn away from the car, I should turn into it!? Who's going to do that? It's like when a child asks you what would happen if he accidentally stopped breathing, and you say, 'Don't worry, you breathe automatically, you can't stop yourself.' He becomes self-conscious about it and by the end of the day he's hyperventilating; I'm doing it now just thinking about it.

# Touch a Tiger

Yes, great idea. Go on, touch a tiger. Because they're beautiful, aren't they? So majestic and powerful. 'What immortal hand or eye could frame thy fearful symmetry?' Quite – even William Blake, the gibbering eighteenth-century fruitcake – knew that tigers can be a bit unpredictable. Ask Siegfried and Roy, or whichever one was half-eaten by their pet tiger, Montecore, what can go wrong if you touch a big stripey cat and he's not in the mood.

Or talk to what's left of the victims of tiger attacks at John Aspinall's zoos, or maybe the guy at San Francisco Zoo who thought it might be fun to dangle his leg over the wall in the face of a Siberian tiger. Except, oh no, you can't, he's dead. All that's left of him is his shoe and the leg they found inside the enclosure.

John Aspinall and all the other nature bonders seem to have lived under the delusion that somehow they could turn back the evolutionary clock to a time when we were all animals together and we walked the same hunting grounds. But over the years, tigers grew sharp teeth and stripy fur and we developed the rudimentary tools, housing and comfortable desk jobs. We don't belong in the same room as a tiger. They are majestic and dazzling animals, and wildlife photographers and cameramen should get paid double for allowing me to look at tigers in the comfort and safety of my well-appointed home. Touching one would be, apart from a dangerous waste of time, an insult to their professionalism.

# Say Hello to a Stranger Every Day

Now, you don't have to be Stephen Hawking to work out why this is a bad idea – nutters. Nutters, nutters everywhere.

There are some idealistic, dreamy people who believe that being more open and friendly to strangers could result in a chance meeting with someone who could change their life. Well, they might be right. Stabbed by a random nutter; how's that for a change?

Even making eye contact with a stranger is risky enough: 'Who are you looking at?' is at the milder end of the range of possible responses. 'Aiiieeee! Another victim for you, Satan!' is the sort of comment you want to avoid.

Maybe 25 years in London have made me paranoid, but in fact rural and small-town England is the preferred stomping ground for really dangerous nutters. Hanging round the Walberswick bus stop or shuffling about in a Northampton shopping precinct is a nutter just waiting for that fateful handshake.

Can it really be that dangerous? Well, look at the statistics. Every year there are 36,000 random murders, and 85 per cent are committed by nutters who reacted badly to being asked to shake hands by a stranger. Or something like that.

And just suppose your handshakee turns out to be non-lethal and quite friendly, but boring and unshake-offable. This often happens on holiday when people smile and nod at each other in the dining room or the bar and bingo! Just like that, your holiday is ruined. They will start asking what your plans are for the next day and suggesting you sit together at dinner. You will be left with two options: either counteract your early friendliness with extreme rudeness, or initiate a routine of lies, dodges and tail-shaking that Sam Spade would be proud of.

The die-hard optimist and romantic will ask: 'What about eyes meeting across a crowded room and love at first sight? Nothing ventured, nothing gained.' OK, it's true; if you were to avoid random meetings at all costs and only have intercourse (of any kind) with people you already know, you may as well live in a closed community of monks or sign up to an arranged marriage. There is a one in a billion chance that the stranger you randomly shake hands with could be THE ONE, the perfect soulmate; someone who could make you complete, be your better half, bring the best out of you, make you more fully, truly, really you and transform your life in an amaaazing, dolphin-rubbing sort of way. But probably not though, eh?

# Look into a Child's Eyes, See Yourself and Smile

● ● ● ● ● ● ● ● ● ● ● ● ● ● ● ● ● ● ● ● ● ● ● ● ● ● ● ● ● ● ● ● ● ● ● ●

This ambition – a genuine listing from a well-used '101 Things To Do' website – has the same emetic effect on me as those slogans about 'stopping to smell the flowers' or 'taking a swim in Lake YOU'.

To anyone who thinks this might be a good idea and is unaware of some basic facts of life, I'd like to point out that:

**a.** children do actually turn into adults, and
**b.** you were actually once a child yourself.

So there's really no reason to go around pestering or frightening little children saying, 'Come on, hold still. I'm trying to look into your eyes and see myself.' Instead, find a photo taken when you were, say, five or six, and look at it for a bit and recognise that it is in fact yourself and, if you feel like it, smile or just go, 'Oh yeah, that's me.'

As daft as it sounds, this ambition isn't so far removed from those intrepid voyages of discovery to places like the Himalayas: you reach the top of your snowy peak, look down and suddenly realise how insignificant, how unimportant you are in the scheme of things. Then you come home and insist on hogging dinner-party conversations with endless self-important tales of your humbling experience.

Recognising yourself in the eyes of a child is just like this because – do you see? – it's a journey of *self*-discovery. But the trouble with self-discovery is that the next step is always 'being true to yourself'. This is supposed to be a very good thing, although it basically boils down to 'doing what you like', which leads with grim inevitability to 'expressing yourself', i.e. telling us stuff we don't want to know. Feelings, emotions, loves, hates, fears, desires – great torrents of crap come tumbling out into the waiting arms of Trisha and Jeremy Kyle. Forget self-discovery, whatever happened to self-restraint and self-control? Not enough people repress their emotions these days. There's a lot to be said for bottling it all up.

In the 21st century people spend so much time looking for themselves in the eyes of children or experiencing 'steep learning curves' of self-discovery on reality television that an entire market has sprouted to service selfishness – businesses like MEtime, myHotel and MySpace. An Internet search for sites with 'Me' or 'My' in the title yields 2.1 billion results. That'll soon be one for every person on the planet, which has a frightening symmetry about it.

We used to worry about a future where Big Brother would be watching us. More likely no one will be watching anybody but themselves and Big Brother will be looking up his own arse.

# Be Totally Honest with Your Partner

When did *that* ever work? Relationships are built on dishonesty, mistrust and poor communication. How many couples would have split up in the first few weeks if the question 'Do you fancy going to see that Werner Herzog film?' was answered truthfully? As relationships develop it's 'Do you prefer my hair long or short?', 'Shall I ask my parents down this weekend?' and then the killer: 'Which of the actresses in this film do you fancy?' To which the right answer is, 'The one who looks most like you.'

The early stages of a relationship are dressed up as 'mystery' and 'spark' and part of 'a wonderful voyage of discovery' or more simply – getting to know someone, with the obvious proviso that you must never get to know someone properly, or it will all get boring. It's the same with people who feel compelled to move house when they've done absolutely everything doable to their current property. If you like where you live, the trick is to never finish it.

Here's another sweeping, sexist-but-true statement – the urge for truthfulness in a relationship always comes from the woman. Perhaps that's because, for centuries, men have been fairly duplicitous and unreliable with women, although if you ask a man what's wrong he will never say 'nothing'.

It is true to say, though, that when it comes to relationships men are only after one thing – yes, an easy life. An easy life means avoiding intense situations, agreeing that the Vanilla Bean paint is better than the Almond White, not venturing to suggest that Victoria Beckham looks quite pretty sometimes and avoiding the truth if it's going to lead to trouble such as not speaking, crying, fighting, stabbing, etc.

One of the most appalling television programmes ever, *Mistresses*, contains a classic scene in which one woman, who has shagged a bloke at work and got pregnant, wants to pretend it's her husband's baby to spare him the pain, but of course her friends advise her that she shouldn't deceive him: 'It's better to tell him the truth – you owe it to him'. What? Owe it to him to make him miserable, insanely jealous and possibly homicidal?

'He hung my lover upside down from a meat hook but that's better than living a lie.'

Have these people never read any literature? Don't they know about Cordelia in *King Lear*?

'How much do you love me, Cordelia?'

'The usual amount, given that I'm your daughter.'

'Aaaaaargh! Rage blow and crack your cheeks, you cataracts etc.'

Several deaths, an eye-gouging and a suicide or two later, Cordelia's dead, but thank goodness she was honest.

*Tess of the D'Urbervilles* is a book I refer to often. In fact, if I wasn't ideologically opposed to the concept, I'd say it was a book you absolutely must read before you die. Tess is the sort of girl to whom bad things happen. On the night of her wedding to

Angel, a man she is deeply in love with, she confesses needlessly to her seduction by the novel's villain. On hearing this, Angel dumps her. She then falls on hard times and ends up being hanged for murder. Admittedly, Hardy thought we were all doomed anyway, but clearly his point here is that it's better to keep schtum in certain romantic situations, and how many times is this borne out in everyday life?

I think this philosophy is best expressed in the lyrics of a Divine Comedy song, 'Sticks and stones may break my body/ Words can tear me apart'. Tearing someone else apart is a heck of a thing to risk doing, just so you can tick a box on a list next to the item that reads 'Be totally honest with your partner'.

# Drink Champagne out of a Slipper

This has a Gay Paris, *fin de siècle*, *joie de vivre* appeal about it, the kind of thing Marilyn Monroe would do with Laurence Olivier in *The Prince and the Showgirl*, or Jack Lemmon and Shirley MacLaine in *Irma La Douce* (something for the teenagers, there). Anyway, this is all about spontaneity and gaiety and romantic moonlit walks in a glamorous city by a river.

Picture the scene. Your top hat is at a jaunty angle, your bow tie undone as you swing the champagne bottle in one hand and tease your date with the other. She tosses her head back, laughing at all your jokes, and teeters along on her heels until, blissfully fatigued, she flops down on a bench close by a cheeky old busking accordionist, playing 'Clair de Lune' with a look in his eye that says, 'Ah! What it is to be young!'

She kicks off her expensive slippers and you slump beside her – you'd both love more champagne; she picks up one slipper and playfully holds it towards the bottle – '*Pourquoi non?*' What the hell! – this is a once-in-a-lifetime moment you will remember forever, but . . . oh dear! As the slipper comes within range of your nose you realise that a long and lively evening of cocktails and dancing has taken its toll on her feet. Cracked skin, hard heels – those fashionable shoes come with a price. There's a sticking plaster on her little toe, another one on the back of her ankle and a hint of Parmesan in the air. Still, don't let it spoil the moment! You tip the bottle carefully but it's tricky in this light and that shoe isn't exactly watertight. The Bollinger keeps spilling out, and as she tips the slipper to drink, it becomes clear that there's a design flaw in this process. Champagne dribbles down her chin, down her cleavage and all over the front of a rather expensive gown.

'Oh shit, I'm sorry, er . . . it was my fault.'

'Have you got a handkerchief?'

'No, but it'll come out. I'll take it to the dry cleaners myself.'

'Actually, I really am a bit damp now.'

'Oh no!'

'Were you that desperate for a drink?'

'Eh? But you wanted—'

'I'm going to have to get changed. I probably should make a move anyway.'

'Shall I walk you home?'

'No, it's OK, I'll get a cab . . . I'll call you next week.'

If only she'd just had a swig out of the bottle you might have got a shag out of it.

# Go Speed Dating

Do you remember when your mum would say, 'You're not going to the Pig and Leper tonight, are you? It's a right cattle market, is that.' Well, that's what speed dating is. A herd of human livestock hoping to cop off. You may have tried it already – it's a big business now – so why does it appear on lists of things to do before you die? Well, if you *don't* know much about it, it's quite an intense evening and it's impossible to avoid speaking to a member of the opposite sex. It's really for people who are cautious and have trouble plucking up the courage to approach someone and ask them for a date. Everyone at the event is theoretically in the same predicament as each other, although so many reviews have been written of speed-dating evenings that you'd have to assume at least half the people at any given event are journalists at work.

On the *Can't Be Arsed* MTTIW calculus (More Trouble Than It's Worth) it scores pretty well – you don't have to travel far, you can find somewhere local doing a speed-dating evening pretty easily; you stand around having a Smirnoff Ice or Bacardi Breezer, chat to someone at random for a few minutes, then everyone moves on to the next person. It's a bit like a dance up at the big house in a Jane Austen novel, where all the ladies have their cards marked by hopeful gentlemen. At the end of the speed-dating evening, if anyone has given you reason to think they fancy a foxtrot, you get the organisers to sort you out a proper date with them. There's little fuss, little risk, and the rewards might be great.

So what's the catch? To put it simply, it's twenty quid a time. Good ideas always pay out to someone and there are some companies operating regular speed-dating nights throughout Britain who have customers literally stuffing money through their letterbox. It was a Jewish man – now a rabbi – who set up the first ever speed-dating service to enable Jews to date other Jews, and he's the one who owns the trademark. He now writes books about how to speed-date and scores of other entrepreneurs have jumped on the gravy train. This puts a completely different complexion on speed dating. If I am now forking out twenty quid for the chance to chat to fifteen or twenty women for five minutes each, I begin to question the evening's value for money. The MTTIW calculus now has to factor in cost and I begin to weigh up the relative attractiveness of the sample of women attendees against the cash outlay. This is bound to affect my conversation – I become more cautious, reserved, even rude, to the point where I might actually raise the issue of cost versus attractiveness to some of the women I'm talking to. Inevitably I rate poorly with these women and I get no follow-up calls from anyone. The twenty quid is not only wasted, it has itself contributed to its own wasting. The whole edifice crumbles like a house of cards and reluctantly I have to recommend that you avoid speed dating.

# Go Dating with Your Mum (Speed or Otherwise)

Do you remember Fergie? Sarah, the Duchess of York, who was married to a prince but was photographed sucking a bald man's toe? She appeared in the papers quite recently with her daughters, declaring that they often hit the town together 'on the pull'. When she was a premier league royal it was always said that Fergie had the 'common touch', but this takes the cake. It's the sort of thing Elsie Tanner might have been accused of in *Coronation Street* as evidence that she was 'no better than she should be'. It conjures up the terrible image of a late–middle-aged woman having a catfight with her daughter over a bit of rough, or worse, cheering her on in a clinch with a prospective 'good catch'. I don't have any double standards about this – the sight of an old man and his son going out on the pull would probably be even more horrendous. George Best and Cameron? Kingsley and Martin Amis? Prince Philip and Charles?

I imagine the older partner in the double act is trying to prove that they've still 'got it', a bit like in those fashion spreads in weekend newspapers where the fashion editor appears with her teenage daughter wearing the same clothes from Top Shop; '. . . but which one of us is the teenager?' is the implied question. 'The one without the moustache!' is the usual reply.

But what could be going through the mind of the younger partner? Do they console themselves with the knowledge that at least they are somehow 'bonding' in a meaningful way with Mum/Dad? Well, they could do that by going round to see them for lunch on Sunday or taking them for a drive to a nice stately home or a browse round a garden centre or by just ringing them up and saying 'I love you'. Just once.

Maybe your parents aren't pensioners, maybe they're Grey Pounders or Silver Surfers or Goodtime Charlies or whatever the ad men call them now. Maybe they'd love to go out on the pull with you to Revolution or Yates's Wine Lodge and have a proper night out like young people do. Do you really want to see your beloved mummy spilling out of her boob tube and puking up in a gutter, or your dad rubbing himself up against a stupefied off-duty nurse or jostling someone in a minicab queue? You must resist or you will not respect each other in the morning.

# Have a Threesome

This is supposed to be every man's fantasy. I can't imagine it's a woman's fantasy any more than that other great prize for sexual adventurers – occasionally described as 'bowling from the pavilion end', or more brutally as 'one up the bum, no harm done'. It seems these arrangements exist purely for a man to tick off a list with his mates. The only time you'll ever read about or hear a woman saying how much she loves threesomes or anal sex is in a lads' mag or on a dodgy late-night Channel 5 show called something like *Sex Matters for Girls*, which you can guarantee only blokes are watching.

In particular a threesome is the kind of thing fairly aggressive and dominant men try to force on a timid partner, who is usually too worried to resist in case the man abandons her. Or it involves professional footballers assembled in such numbers that the woman has no option but to submit – the tabloids call it 'roasting' but most people would call it gang rape.

For the man who won't go quite as far as a gang rape with his work colleagues, the conventional threesome is simply a massive ego trip – two women who are so consumed with desire for him that they'll share him with another woman, and will 'put on a show' for him with each other while he recovers. Men who try and convince their partners into joining in with their scheme often employ the lamest excuse ever: 'It will revive our flagging relationship', which, as excuses go, is right up there with 'I have an addictive personality', 'I've been under a lot of stress recently' and 'I was holding it for an older boy'.

Actually I can't see the appeal of any kind of physical union with a woman where someone else is in the room. Especially another bloke. Let's be honest, you are likely to be looking into another man's face while you're crashing the custard van – it's either going to be acutely embarrassing or ridiculous or plain weird, and not in any way arousing. The threesome involving two women is also fraught with logistical problems. Prostitutes say (so I'm told) that the man who pays for two women is not thinking straight because at any one time one of the women is doing nothing – either watching TV or filing her nails. How awkward is that? And I have to say, what a terrible waste of money.

The threesome, like a lot of spicing up of love lives, is a function of becoming bored with 'conventional' sex. But how much do you have to get to become bored of it? Despite what they boast in magazine surveys, I'll bet most people are way off the required amount for boredom to ensue.

Some people claim they are genetically disposed to 'need'

more sex than other people (see excuses above) and there's even a new term for it – 'sex addict' – which allows quacks to set up clinics where 'addicts' can go to 'cure' themselves of their affliction. In the olden days these places were called monasteries and convents. But it's funny how only rich and famous people seem to suffer from sex addiction, whereas poorer, working-class people are not sex addicts, but sex-offenders and rapists.

# Have Sex in an Aeroplane

This reminds me of the teenage boy who sneaked up behind David Cameron, then pretended to sneeze and wipe the snot on his back – the pleasure seems to be entirely bound up in doing something that other people don't know about or wouldn't dare do. Yes, yes, so you had sex in a toilet – well done, you must both be very proud. There's a sketch in the *Armstrong and Miller* TV show where a character in a situation requiring courage, nobility and manliness admits with a self-satisfied grin that he's wearing his wife's knickers – and that just about sums up the appeal of this. The physical pleasure must be minimal – there is not enough room to urinate or defecate in comfort in an aeroplane toilet, never mind make the beast with two backs. Having a cigarette in there afterwards is much more daring – you can probably go to prison for that these days.

# 36

# Have Sex on a Beach

Beaches again! I've already documented my aversion to the X + Beach equation. It's just some sand and some sea, for God's sake! It seems if everybody had their wish, beaches would be so full of people doing things – from lighting fires, watching the sun rise, riding a horse (or riding a horse bareback), to doing ju-jitsu, working out pi to 3,000 places, shagging or having a vasectomy – that there'd be no room for the people who just want to sit on the fucking beach and build a sand castle. Surely with all this activity going on there won't be nearly enough privacy. But – ah! – that's the whole point of this, isn't it? The risk of discovery! It's a bit like dogging and those people who have aeroplane sex, not in a toilet, but under the blankets in first class, although class is the one thing they surely don't have.

We often hear the question, 'Why are we so uptight about

sex? It's perfectly natural.' Yes, and it's perfectly natural to be a bit discreet about it, because it's a fairly intimate thing to do and you have to put yourself in a pretty vulnerable position, physically and emotionally. Can you imagine what it would be like if people were genuinely uninhibited about sex and were boffing each other in public with no regard to the sensitivities of passers-by? It would be like Blackpool on any night of the week. Is that the kind of world you want?

# Have An Affair

● ● ● ● ● ● ● ● ● ● ● ● ● ● ● ● ● ● ● ● ● ● ● ● ● ● ● ● ● ● ● ● ●

What absolute bollocks. Having an affair is the ultimate waste of time and probably the very definition of the phrase 'more trouble than it's worth'. Just how complicated do you want your life to be? All that planning, all the complex timetables and scheduling that goes into utterly deceiving someone you live with. The kind of evasion and lies required to cheat on a partner successfully would not disgrace a top-of-the-range serial killer.

Then again, you could always not bother with the deceit and the elaborate excuses. Some people will come over all noble in the midst of their philandering and say something like, 'I owe it to my wife to tell her the truth.' Oh really? More than you owed it to her not to shag someone else behind her back? We often hear of the 'thrill of being found out' as one of the motivating factors for having an affair in the first place, but I don't buy that. I'd say the constant dread of exposure would totally obliterate whatever quick thrills were on offer. How good would the sex have to be to make it worth all that palaver?

And then there's the expense involved. Come on, those love nests don't come cheap, if my tabloid newspapers are anything to go by. It seems that any self-respecting love rat has to shell out at least £250,000 for a decent love nest in which to 'romp'. Then there are all the slap-up chicken dinners that have to be bought, not to mention the champagne, chocolates, baby oil and all the other phrases that *News of the World* reporters have ready to cut and paste. It's all bound to mount up, and credit-card statements are even more of a giveaway to an inquisitive spouse than the 'Sent Items' on the texting menu.

The other major cost, of course, is to your dignity. Most men tend to have affairs just when they've reached the age for the whole process to be physically degrading for themselves; that's any time between 35 and death. Sagging belly, muscle-wastage, greying pubes, nasal hair, yellowy feet, elasticated-sock imprint on the lower leg, hideous teeth, lack of stamina, feeble erections – what do they think they look like? And yet one of the most often cited reasons for a man to 'look elsewhere' is the desire to prove he's 'still got it'. But can any man really hear himself saying that out loud without everyone else laughing?

Let's not forget either, the risk of being quite seriously stabbed or poisoned or shot or otherwise killed or maimed by a scorned lover. When one half of a couple cheats on the other with a third person, there is, by the devilish laws of mathematics, always going to be at least one person feeling pretty bad about the whole thing. If the secret lover is also cheating on *their* partner, it's going to get pretty bloody and you may as well adopt the ancient Roman method for punishing wrongdoers and throw yourself into a sack with a snake, a chicken and a dog.

A favourite excuse men give for infidelity is the one about biological programming. 'I'm biologically programmed to have sex with as many women as possible.' What a brilliant cop-out. This biological programming could explain a lot, like the fiddling with the genitals through the trouser pockets, and the inability to fold clothing or take anything out of the oven without dropping it and screaming, 'Shit, that's hot!'

There's something that doesn't add up about the idea that men who have affairs are only obeying some kind of natural instinct. What about man's instinctive reluctance to enter into a conversation with *anyone*, least of all a woman? A lot of men I know, if they could deceive their wives into thinking they were working late, would just have a quiet sit-down with a newspaper and a drink. Why on earth would you concoct an elaborate ruse to elude your wife, just so you could spend the rest of the evening talking to another woman? And don't say, 'We wouldn't be doing much talking, mate, know what I mean?' That's bollocks; there's *always* talking. The reason why most men don't read fiction is because they find it difficult enough engaging emotionally with another *person*, never mind some fictional characters, so why on earth would they want to double the problem in real life?

Fans of 'playing away' will argue that it's only once in a while, and if you could get away with it just once you should. I'm never going to buy that argument, because if someone were trying to persuade me to become a hitman or a gentleman jewel-thief, they'd say exactly the same thing.

I've only been talking about men and their affairs here, because I've really no idea why women do anything, although I did read somewhere that they're unfaithful for just two reasons: boredom or revenge. That might not be strictly true, but women often feel they are more likely to be the cheatee than the cheater. They also say that there are double standards when it comes to infidelity. A woman who sleeps around will always be called a slag, while a promiscuous man will always be admired. Well, I don't think there are double standards – for every Casanova or James Bond there are scores of widely recognised real-life cads like John Prescott, James Hewitt or Darren Day; men whose names are seldom used in the same sentence as the word 'admiration'…

# CULTURAL STUFF

The thrust of the book is going to change here for a bit. Rather than overrated experiences, the next chunk is all about overrated films, albums and books.

We often hear complaints that our freedoms are being eroded every day. More and more laws are introduced banning one activity or another; our children are becoming prisoners, on the one hand of anxious parents, on the other, of ASBOs; we have the most CCTV cameras per square mile of any country in the world and we may soon all be forced to carry identity cards. But something else is eroding our freedom – our freedom to decide what stuff we like. Television, magazines, manuals and now the Internet are telling us what films we should see, what books we should read, what hotels we should stay in, what restaurants we should eat in and what music we should buy. Some music comes with instructions on when we should listen to it: '50 great tracks to chill out to'. Do I have to chill out to this music? Can't I do my income tax return to it? Or the washing up? Where did it all start, this cultural imperialism? How did we get from the recommendation of a friend or even a critic to 'If you see one film this weekend you must see . . .'?

I could blame *Desert Island Discs* – a massively popular and iconic radio show that has lasted almost seventy years. It's probably the first ever 'list' show, but the eight records chosen by the 'castaway' have always been peculiar, idiosyncratic, revelatory; never prescriptive. There is no sense that you have missed out or have a hole in your life if you don't like the same stuff. These days the list shows are called things like 'The 100 Best Insects Ever', 'Top 50 Popes', 'The 75 Cheeses You Must Own'. Today everything is either shit or brilliant; there is no in between. *Gavin and Stacey* is brilliant. *Tittybangbang* is terrible. Actually, it is terrible, but the more people go on about how brilliant something is, the less I want to join in. Take *The Simpsons* – it is very good. It's funny and clever and unpredictable. I'd stop there, but the list shows don't – apparently it's the best children's show of all time, the best cartoon ever drawn and the greatest TV programme the world has ever seen. Personally, I prefer *Tom and Jerry*.

Last year was a bumper year for giant lists of things you absolutely must see/hear/read/visit before you die. Here are some of the most overrated . . .

# ALBUMS

# Sgt. Pepper's Lonely Hearts Club Band

● ● ● ● ● ● ● ● ● ● ● ● ● ● ● ● ● ● ● ● ● ● ● ● ● ● ● ● ● ● ● ● ●

I will agree that it's a very influential album that changed pop music, but that doesn't make it great. Aristophanes wrote the first ever comedy but you don't find him on any list of the Top 100 Comedians, and to be honest, a lot of his stuff isn't funny at all – a lot of phallus-waving and single entendres.

On *Sgt. Pepper* there are only three good tracks – 'She's Leaving Home', 'Day in the Life' and the title track, which would have been much better if they hadn't put those silly trumpets on it. 'With a Little Help from My Friends' is a nice enough song, suitable for Val Doonican or Clive Dunn, but not Ringo (and certainly not Joe Cocker). The rest of it is just average to poor. Take 'Within You and Without You'; you'd think the other three would've had enough of George Harrison's sitar doo-da which he'd been inflicting on them since

'Norwegian Wood'. It's like Jools Holland's 'boogie-woogie piano', which he manages to crowbar into every act that appears on *Later* . . . Then there are Lennon's lazy lyrics that he could never be bothered to think up himself, but nicked out of newspapers and bill posters – 'and of course, Henry the Horse is topping the bill'? Great poetry . . .

*Sgt. Pepper* ushered in an era that the baby boomers hoped would never end, but end it did, and we were left with the fag-end of an embarrassing hippy culture and all the merchandising 'concepts' and gimmicks which the Beatles had thrown at the project. The gannets in the music business seized on this stuff and soon everyone was running up massive bills, pissing about for months in recording studios and turning out pompous gatefold concept albums. The Beatles, bless 'em, were only trying to give the record buyers extra value with the elaborate cover art, lyric sheet and free poster. They even left 'Penny Lane' and 'Strawberry Fields Forever' off the album because it was felt to be cheating people to 'pad it out' with singles. Just think, if they had been a bit more cynical, *Sgt. Pepper* could actually have been quite a good record.

# *Dark Side of the Moon*

● ● ● ● ● ● ● ● ● ● ● ● ● ● ● ● ● ● ● ● ● ● ● ● ● ● ● ● ● ● ● ● ● ●

Boooonnngg . . . Biiiiiinnnggg . . . tick tock tick tock tick tock tick tock . . . Boooonnnngggggg . . . Biiiiinnnnnnnggg.

A lot of *Dark Side of the Moon* is like this. There are, as you would expect from musical geniuses, some wonderful spine-tingling moments on the album, but mainly it's long instrumental passages and sustained chords and boring sound effects. It's perfect for hippies to listen to with the lights off, plus the words are about, uh, y'know, generals and politicians and breadheads and stuff. It's funny how rock stars who are signed to multinational record labels and are absolutely minted can write so contemptuously of big business and 'Them'. Look at shy, retiring Buddhist George Harrison – 'Piggies' on the *White Album* is an incredibly snooty condemnation of materialism from the same pen that wrote 'Taxman', complaining about how much tax multimillionaires have to pay. To be completely fair to David Gilmore, and quite a few rich men of his generation, he has given millions to charity. It's also difficult to blame Pink Floyd for the hideous associations this record has for me. One of the worst memories of my teenage years is being stuck at a house party overnight, where Jacqueline Stebbings, my heart's desire, had copped off with Mick Clarkson. Rather than stay in the same room as them while they sucked each other's faces off,

I retreated to a bedroom where some other hippies from my sixth form were, of course, listening to *Dark Side of The Moon* with the lights off. As the only other available music was *Close to the Edge* by Yes, my options were: kill everyone in the house and set fire to it, or try to go to sleep to the shrieks of that woman on 'Great Gig In The Sky'. Meanwhile the hippies discussed the validity of the theory that if you start *Dark Side of the Moon* at the third roar of the MGM Lion, at the beginning of *The Wizard of Oz*, the album becomes a soundtrack for the film. I don't know if that's true but I *am* sure that, if Dante, the poet of *The Inferno* had been alive in the 1970s, this experience would go into his innermost circle of Hell.

# *Thriller*

It's disco music and therefore crap. File under the Bee Gees, the Dooleys or Kelly Marie.

# *Pet Sounds*

• • • • • • • • • • • • • • • • • • • • • • • • • • • • • • • • • • • • •

This is a classic example of an 'An All Time Top 50' album that everyone feels obliged to buy but never really listens to. If they did, it would lose its classic status overnight. I have at least three copies of *Pet Sounds* – one vinyl and two on CD. I suffered an attack of that particular brand of amnesia that affects middle-aged men with too many possessions. The first CD was a replacement of my vinyl copy and the second was just a mistake – I played it so rarely, I'd just forgotten I had it. But you know how it is – you're in a record shop, you see Pet Sounds for £4.99 and say to your self: 'a classic album for under a fiver?!' and the self-deception is complete. Because of its legendary status, *Pet Sounds* was the very first album I loaded into my iPod and it was such a faff to manually type all the track listings, I couldn't be arsed to add another album for six months. So in the end, I got to know *Pet Sounds* pretty well.

Even with the advantage of saturation air-play in my house, *Pet Sounds* never failed to irritate. As with *Sgt. Pepper*, there are a few decent tracks on it; you can't knock 'God Only Knows' and 'I Just Wasn't Made For These Times' but, again like *Sgt. Pepper*, the album is massively over-produced. Some of the sounds on it are just wrong and in some places the musicians are being forced to play in the wrong key; it's a wilful tunelessness. Brian

Wilson went a bit loopy making this album and almost took a load of other people with him, including me. Listen to the ridiculous harmonicas on 'I Know There's An Answer' – they sound like the incidental music to a terrible 50s sitcom like *The Navy Lark*, or something – or the middle bit in the otherwise quite pleasing 'Let's Go Away For A While'. But the main problem with *Pet Sounds* is that it's a Beach Boys record: there's no escape from those voices or those puke-inducing harmonies: at the beginning of 'Don't Talk' they are like the aural equivalent of that combination of smell, taste and texture you find in a gaudy bed-and-breakfast toilet – all vicious pink shag-pile carpet and cloying air freshener.

I have had the benefit of being bombarded by this album for an extremely long time, so my hatred of it has been carefully cultivated, but if even half of the people who had bought it, because Mojo, Rolling Stone and Q Magazine polls had named it one of the best albums ever, had ever listened to it for ten minutes, there might well be civil unrest, leading to the defenestration of pollsters and rock journalists.

# *Blonde on Blonde*

• • • • • • • • • • • • • • • • • • • • • • • • • • • • • • • • • • • •

Bob Dylan can't sing or play the harmonica and reminds me of the near-certifiable chemistry student I once shared a house with. I suppose I can't blame Bob for that, but you have to ask, is there a single song written by Dylan that hasn't been recorded better by someone else? Even the Seekers' version of 'The Times They Are a-Changin'' tops the original. And I reckon a starving Ethiopian would have made a better fist of his line on 'We Are The World': 'It's true we'll make a better day/ Just you and me-eeeeeee' (apply horrible nasal drone).

Dylan fans insist that the lyrics alone elevate Bob to poet status, but do I want a singing poet? Have you ever been to a Shakespeare production and endured the Hey Nonny Nonny song from the clown? Why don't they just edit those bits out, by the way? No one would notice or care. I haven't the faintest desire to hear a recording of Ted Hughes singing selections from 'Wodwo', or Thomas Hardy crooning 'The Darkling Thrush', or Andrew Motion singing . . . er, whatever he wrote. The nearest I want to get to a singing poet is John Cooper Clarke.

Bob Dylan also introduced the Beatles to dope. Now I'm not a drug user (see No. 77), but I do know the Beatles were making perfectly decent records until he messed with their minds. Yes, someone else would probably have done it if not Dylan, but let's be honest, most of their work after 1964 was of variable quality and very often crap. John Lennon was an authentic no-nonsense rock'n'roller until he met Dylan and started producing feeble copies of his work. With the exception of a few decent songs on *Rubber Soul* and *Revolver*, then 'Strawberry Fields Forever' and 'A Day In The Life', Lennon was finished as a force in popular music. Ironically, after he met the Beatles, Dylan gave up his acoustic guitar and plugged in to an amp, much to the chagrin of his hard-core hippy fans.

But I don't want to condemn Bob just for the effect he had on the Beatles. Let his own work speak for itself. Many lists of 'Best Ever Albums Ever in the History of the World Ever You Simply Must Own' feature *Blonde on Blonde*. *Rolling Stone* magazine calls it one of the greatest rock'n'roll albums ever made. Rock'n'roll !? There's a track on it called 'Sad Eyed Lady of the Lowlands', which is 11 minutes 23 seconds long. Now as the great Noddy Holder once said, no decent rock'n'roll song should be more than three minutes long. Admittedly some of Noddy's are less than three minutes long and still rubbish, but, there is absolutely no excuse for 11 minutes and 23 seconds. After the first couple of plays, once their novelty value has worn off, all long records are appalling – 'Whiter Shade of Pale', 'Bohemian Rhapsody', 'McArthur Park', 'Paranoid Android' and 'Hey Jude', with its interminable football-chant ending. Apart from the inexcusable length, Bob makes the fatal mistake of using the word 'lady' in that tragic, possessive old-fart way, 'Hey, she's my lady'.

This is just about acceptable in 'The Lady Is A Tramp', and Frank Sinatra carries it off because he is a middle-aged swinger, but do you remember Tom Jones making a total spectacle of himself stomping about in stupid leather trousers singing 'She's a laydeah'? It's cringe-making, medallion-wearing, pathetic, posturing, twirly-moustached, Jason King crap; 'One helluva sexy lady' is the sort of thing DLT would say about Suzi Quattro, and it's probably one of the most un-rock'n'roll things you could ever do. But Bob keeps doing it: see 'Lay, Lady, Lay' on the equally dreary *Nashville Skyline*.

What else is there on this album to give it such elevated status? Ah yes, 'Rainy Day Women' – you've probably heard that one; it's pathetic. 'Everybody must get stoned.' He means *'stoned'*, y'know, like on drugs, tee-hee.

Then there's 'Just Like a Woman', which is supposed to be the most popular track. It starts off a bit like a proper song and Bob even does a bit of what most people would recognise as proper singing, but then, oh dear . . . all that stuff about her making love 'like a woman' but breaking 'like a little girl'. Did someone say his lyrics were poetry?

How about 'Visions of Johanna'? Again, it's hard to get past the intro with the terrible harmonica sounding like a dreadful one-man band – remember Don Partridge, anyone? 'Sweet Marie' sounds promising, but why bother going to all the trouble to get a decent band in and rehearse them if you're going to piss all over their stuff with that dreadful droning? Someone should have told him his talent lay elsewhere – picture-framing or upholstery, maybe. Honestly, if you haven't heard much of his stuff, which I haven't, you can give Bob Dylan a wide berth with a clean conscience.

# *Nevermind*

No one could argue that 'Smells Like Teen Spirit' isn't a great record. As soon as I heard it I wanted to get the album. I was still clinging to the belief that CDs were a passing fad so I bought it on vinyl, which probably explains why I never bothered listening to the rest of it. Teen Spirit is Track 1 and after that it's pretty thin gruel. Skipping tracks on vinyl is not easy if 'Can't Be Arsed' is your motto, so after 'Teen Spirit' I would just take the record off. After a few listens I just stopped bothering with it altogether.

Then, years later, I paid £4.99 for the CD version and I realised the truth – I was right the first time. 'Come As You Are' and 'Lithium' are pretty good, but the rest of the material follows a basic formula – a quiet bit followed by a shouty bit. I believe this is what is known as grunge: possibly the most pointless musical/tribal movement ever. What does it stand for? Nothing. What do grunge people wear? Check shirts and ripped jeans; dresses with Doc Martens for the chicks – er, that's it. What other grunge bands are there? Soundgarden, Pearl Jam and Alice in Chains. Hardly Merseybeat, is it? When *Time* magazine, which loves to spot a trend, had difficulty pinning down who exactly was buying grunge music, it settled on the suitably ill-defined Generation X.

'This group of 18 to 29-year-olds is hardly recognised as a

social force or even noticed much at all.' Yep, that just about sums it up.

This searing insight appeared in the late 80s – a particularly dreadful time for music and quite a dreary period throughout the world generally, apart from the fall of the Berlin wall and the collapse of communism. The most intriguing social phenomenon at the time involved people sitting on sofas drinking overpriced coffee. Coincidentally, like grunge, the overpriced coffee boom started in Seattle. What a damning indictment of a town – the home of grunge and Starbucks!

Nirvana were lucky no one else was making even half-decent records at the time or with anywhere near as much passion. But what's so great about passion? At the end of the day, what you've got is a long-haired scruffy bloke screaming and shouting a lot. Roger Daltry and Robert Plant proved how tedious that can be.

So how did it get to the point where Nirvana and Kurt Cobain are revered almost like gods? Well, the shotgun suicide didn't hurt and he left behind a grieving girlfriend to tend to the legend, who made Yoko Ono seem the model of decorum and restraint. He also left behind a drummer called Dave Grohl, a funny, cheeky, light-hearted little fellow who must have found it a bit of a strain hanging out with Kurt. He went on to make many more and better albums with the Foo Fighters than he ever did with Nirvana, proving that the singing drummer can be tolerated if you give him his own band. Why aren't the Foo Fighters on any lists?

# *Electric Ladyland*

OK, so Jimi Hendrix made the lead guitar cool. Or was that Eddie Cochrane or Scotty Moore or Cliff Gallup or Chuck Berry or Muddy Waters or John Lee Hooker or Dick Dale or Peter Green or Link Wray?

The way some people talk about Hendrix you'd think he'd invented the electric guitar. What he did was pop up out of nowhere in mid-60s London and do some astonishingly original things with his instrument, of which playing it with his teeth and setting fire to it were the least impressive. But despite two or three decent records – 'Purple Haze' and three tracks on *Electric Ladyland*: 'Voodoo Child (Slight Return)', 'Crosstown Traffic' and 'All Along the Watchtower' (another Dylan song done better than Dylan) – Hendrix's major achievement appears to have been turning the guitar into a giant cock.

Lead guitarists need little encouragement when it comes to self-indulgence – it's their natural disposition. The phallic nature of the guitar was exploited from the early days of rock'n'roll, and no doubt interminable, noodly blues solos from a man with a guitar had been annoying other musicians for fifty years before Hendrix came along. But he enshrined the art of musical masturbation in monumentally tedious works like 'Voodoo Chile' (over fifteen minutes long) and those legendary live performances in which he appeared in flowing robes like some kind of Great Wizard with his magic wand – a sort of musical equivalent of Ali Bongo. He was a fantastically talented musician and terrific showman, but whenever I hear his music I react like Emperor Joseph II to Mozart's *Marriage of Figaro* – 'Very impressive but too many notes'. Far from making the lead guitar cool, Hendrix encouraged the likes of Eric Clapton, Jimmy Page, Ritchie Blackmore, Eddie Van Halen and Carlos Santana to unleash their worst excesses on a baffled public, and although there are lots of people who like that sort of thing and vote *Electric Ladyland* as one of the greatest ever, I'm afraid you could listen to it a hundred times and still not remember more than a couple of decent tunes from it.

# *The Velvet Underground and Nico*

Rock-magazine polls make this number seven in the 'best album of all time' chart. I doubt many people have actually listened to it, they've just seen the cover and nodded knowingly: 'Ah yes, this was Warhol's art project, wasn't it?' It's the rubbish drawing of a banana on the cover that reminds you of the Andy Warhol connection and makes you want to throw the thing on the floor and stamp on it before you've even heard it.

The massively overrated Andy Warhol is credited with 'producing' this album and gets a name check on the front cover underneath his banana drawing, when all he did was pay $1,500 for the recording studio hire and stand near the band while they mumbled their way through some pretty ordinary material. Most of the stuff, including 'Heroin' and 'Waiting for the Man' consists of Lou Reed's sub-Dylan drone (as if the real thing isn't bad enough) tediously extended over two chords of ham-fisted guitaring. John Cale makes things worse with a viola that sounds like a set of bagpipes, but that's OK because it's art. Then there's Nico – the prototype Model Turned Actress, foisted on the Velvet Underground by Warhol, who actually sounds like a bored waitress, or maybe Phoebe from *Friends* singing 'Smelly Cat'. If Kate Moss or Naomi Campbell started making records they would quite rightly be ridiculed and pilloried for over-reaching themselves or for proving how shallow the entertainment business is, but Nico is art and Warhol is a genius. By some kind of accident Nico's appalling backing vocals make 'Sunday Morning' sound quite pleasant, but that's about all I can stomach from this album.

Of course, it's terribly influential, in that it allowed many more poets and artists to stick their noses into rock'n'roll and sell records on the basis of what books they claimed to have read. Brian Eno once said, 'Everyone who bought a copy [of *The VU and Nico*] went on to form a band.' Yes, and I bet they all thought the most important thing about their band was that they had a good slideshow.

# *Exile on Main Street*

. . . . . . . . . . . . . . . . . . . . . . . . . . . . . . . . . . .

The Rolling Stones are brilliant, aren't they? Rough rock'n'roll diamonds compared to those teddy bears of pop, the Beatles. But, oh dear, they didn't have any tunes. All attitude and no melody; all mouth and no trousers. OK, so they did have trousers, but not much more except riffs and licks and only a handful of passable records in over forty years.

That's the other problem with the Rolling Stones – they just will not stop and nobody seems prepared to point out that they look ridiculous; they're over sixty years old, for God's sake.

'Yes, but doesn't Mick look good for his age?'

No – he didn't look good for his age when he was twenty.

'But what about Keef, eh? Hurr hurr! He takes so many drugs he can hardly speak, hurr hurr! He's such a survivor, isn't he?'

Well, he may have survived but he's actually more like a tramp with savings.

*Exile on Main Street* is meant to be the Rolling Stones' best work, but Mick Jagger actually thought it sounded lousy and was, to quote him – 'really not good'. To be fair to Mick, Keith Richards was pretty much in charge for most of the recording; he's supposed to be the authentic rock'n'roller in the band, but it doesn't help this album rise above the mundane. Even one of the most popular tracks, 'Happy', which was recorded without most of the rest of the Stones, is a fairly tedious and predictable song. In fact, you could take the intro of virtually any Rolling Stones track, cut it on to the verse of another one, and never tell the difference – bit of guitar, the drums come in with the bass, Mick Jagger shouts over the top of it, something like 'Mamma baby New Orleans sugar night time woman', boring guitar solo, back to the beginning, repeat to fade. This album is regarded not only as the Stones' best work, but also a rock'n'roll masterpiece. Yet it took a rock critic called Robert Christgau 25 listens to the album before he realised how good it was – *25 listens*!? It's over an hour long. What's this book called? *Can't Be Arsed.*

# *Never Mind the Bollocks Here's The Sex Pistols*

● ● ● ● ● ● ● ● ● ● ● ● ● ● ● ● ● ● ● ● ● ● ● ● ● ● ● ● ● ● ● ● ● ●

OK, so there's 'Pretty Vacant', 'Anarchy in the UK' and 'God Save the Queen'. All brilliant, and probably the best that punk rock could manage. The Damned were a novelty band – frankly, Russ Abbott could have fronted them – and the Clash (see below) sounded like drunks. The rest of punk rock was totally forgettable and as embarrassing in retrospect as Alvin Stardust and Duran Duran. It was only the professional hack-work of Cook and Jones that lifted the Sex Pistols above the ordinary, and even then, all they were playing was heavy metal with an angry man shouting over the top.

At least compared to *Never Mind* by Nirvana, *Never Mind the Bollocks* was genuinely influential, although not necessarily in a good way. The dross that followed the Damned, the Clash and the Sex Pistols were only redeemed by the next wave – the Buzzcocks, the Undertones, Elvis Costello, Squeeze and Blondie; bands with proper songs, who were allowed to sneak on to the radio in the general melee.

Without the Sex Pistols there would have been no punk, it's true, but that doesn't mean this is a classic album any more than the tartan bum-flap is a classic piece of tailoring.

# London Calling

● ● ● ● ● ● ● ● ● ● ● ● ● ● ● ● ● ● ● ● ● ● ● ● ● ● ● ● ● ● ● ● ● ● ● ●

The title track of this album is a cracker, but I don't know how the Clash came up with it because the rest of their stuff is terrible. I'm in dangerous territory here because for some middle-aged men, to insult the Clash is like ripping the ear off their favourite childhood teddy bear. The Clash have shouty choruses so it reminds a lot of men of their early youth, walking round the playground in a gang of mates shouting, 'All-join-on-to-play-at-war!' You can sing this along to most Clash records.

The Clash were as guilty as all the other early punk bands of sounding like drunks or mentals in a shopping precinct but as they grew in popularity and made a bit of money, they were allowed enough time in a studio to experiment with all kinds of drivel. There are a couple of reasonable rockers here like 'Brand New Cadillac' and 'Death or Glory' but I've no idea what you'd call songs like 'Koka Kola' and 'Revolution Rock'. The bonehead pro-terrorist politics of 'Spanish Bombs' would make a sixth-former blush, but then with stuff like 'Rudie Can't Fail' and 'The Guns of Brixton' we see the Clash continue to fanny around with one of the most cringe-making musical genres of all time – white reggae. 'Bank Robber' and 'White Man in Hammersmith Palais' (neither on this album) were two of the worst examples of it, but by being one of the first punk bands to make white reggae appear cool, they gave Sting (shudder!) and the Police some very bad ideas. Joe Strummer seems to have thought the only way he, as the son of a diplomat who went to boarding school, could get 'down' with black people was to play their music. It's a bit patronising to start with but when you perform it so badly, it becomes an insult. It's not an exaggeration to say that a more successful attempt at a black/white crossover was made by Rick Astley with Stock Aitken Waterman.

# *Astral Weeks*

• • • • • • • • • • • • • • • • • • • • • • • • • • • • • • • • • • • •

Van Morrison's masterpiece, according to the critics, may disappoint his fans, as it doesn't contain the popular tunes – no 'Brown Eyed Girl', no 'Jackie Wilson Said', no 'Moondance'. Not that I'm crazy about those songs particularly, or Van

Morrison, for that matter. One of the most annoying things about him is this nickname – 'The Man'. Why is he The Man? I'm not accepting him as The Man just because it rhymes with Van. I don't know if he had anything to do with it himself – but he's certainly done nothing to discourage it. It reminds me of Paul Ince, the former Manchester United midfielder, who insisted on being called 'The Guvnor', although no one bothered. I think we should stop bothering with 'The Man'. Probably too late now.

Anyway, *Astral Weeks* has been described as 'a lyrical song-cycle, somewhere between blues, folk and jazz'. If ever there was an invitation to dislike something, that's it. It seems to be a very personal collection of love songs and impressions of places very significant to him; so personal that it encourages Van Morrison to growl and wail and bawl even more than he does normally, and somehow this is supposed to be a good thing. The trouble with highly personal albums like this is you end up having to listen to ramblings and streams of consciousness about stuff you're not really bothered about.

Take 'Cyprus Avenue' – it's about a girl he fancies in a posh part of town, and I'm afraid there's more of that embarrassing 'Lady' stuff: 'Lord, here comes my lady, rainbow ribbons in her hair.' 'Slim Slow Slider' is three minutes of shouting, groaning and moaning; annoyingly repetitive and reminiscent of the sort of pub musician on 'music night' who can easily ruin your evening because you have to keep turning round and frowning at him in the really shouty bits, and you're just praying for the landlord to say, 'That's enough, son'. But at least 'Slim Slow Slider' lasts only 3 minutes 20 seconds; there's a track on the album called 'Madame George' which is 9 minutes long, and two others that break the 7-minute barrier. According to one critic, on this album, Van 'The Man' manages to 'stretch the notion of "a song" to the limit'. You're telling me. He stretches it so much my patience snapped and I really couldn't be arsed to listen to any more . . .

# Low

●●●●●●●●●●●●●●●●●●●●●●●●●●●●●●●●●●●●●●●●

This album is OK – certainly not terrible – but it's been elevated to a ridiculously high status because it was recorded in Berlin in the bleak mid-70s where everything was moody and 'post-industrial' (that's a good thing?).

The puzzlingly lofty reputation of *Low* and the rest of the 'Berlin Trilogy' is comparable to the position of Bowie himself as a 'great artist'. I'm going out on a limb here but I reckon he's only made five great records – 'Life on Mars', 'Starman', 'Changes', 'Young Americans' and 'Ashes to Ashes'. The rest are all either pretty good to average to rubbish to 'Let's Dance' (the Serious Moonlight, indeed!).

For some reason we are meant to admire Bowie's multiple personas, as if his position as the official Chameleon of Rock is something all rising stars should aspire to. He was at various times, David Jones, David Bowie, Ziggy Stardust, Aladdin Sane, The Man Who Fell To Earth, The Thin White Duke – he's like a kid who's fallen into a dressing-up box. But why should he be applauded for this when that other 70s icon, Mike Yarwood, is long-forgotten? Mike had loads of identities – a quick ruffle of the hair and he was Ken Dodd, a porkpie hat turned him into Eddie Waring, and a simple pair of glasses transformed him into Robin Day or Eric Morecambe. Where's the acclaim for Mike Yarwood?

In fairness to *Low*, a lot of the tracks are under three minutes, but they are pretty pedestrian at best, particularly 'Be My Wife' and 'Breaking Glass', which contains one of the most banal lyrics since the invention of ink – 'Don't look at the carpet/ I threw something awful on it.'

The album's second side (to anyone under 25: look it up) is full of cold, de-humanised instrumentals that the critics call 'glacial', and most of it was shaped by the Grand Poo-Ba of knob-twiddling, Brian Eno, mucking about while Bowie was out of the studio. So we are deprived, if that is the right word, of that weird, almost self-parodying voice of Bowie's, that stark alien-cum-robot timbre, which Gary Numan and the rest of the numanoids – welded to their synthesizers and sci-fi novels – took for their inspiration.

Like a lot of 'best ever albums', *Low* is feted for its huge influence on others, but I could certainly have done without some of the gloomy rubbish Joy Division turned out (they were originally named Warsaw after the depressing instrumental on *Low*) and the pretentious new-romantic dirges of Steve Strange and early Spandau Ballet. It's hard to reconcile the cheeky chappie David Bowie of today with the pale-faced mardy-bum of the mid-70s. His willingness to send himself up and appear in sitcoms these days makes me wonder whether he could even bear to be reminded of that tour during which he'd promised to perform the songs his fans had requested in a poll, apart from the one which attracted by far the most votes, 'The Laughing Gnome'.

# FILMS

# *Citizen Kane*

Like a lot of films, it's terrific in parts; in others it's deadly dull. The opening really draws you in and the first hour is a great fast-forward through an extraordinary life, but come on, that bit with the opera singer and the clapping: who doesn't make a cup of tea when that bit's on? And Orson Welles' old-man make-up is terrible: he's got a joke-shop bald wig on and a cushion under his shirt. Media Studies graduates and film buffs take comments like this incredibly personally, as if by casting doubt on the pure, unadulterated genius of *Citizen Kane* you are somehow insulting their mothers. But I'm not saying it's a terrible film; it's just not the greatest ever made (I don't believe there is such a thing) and it's probably not even the greatest film Orson Welles ever made. *A Touch of Evil* is better and *Citizen Kane* will have to make do with being just pretty good. I know Orson Welles was only about five when he made it, and he dug trenches for the cameras and filmed ceilings and told things in flashback yadda yadda, and maybe no one else had done that before, but really, no one should feel like they have leprosy if they haven't seen it.

# *Battleship Potemkin*

If you can get past the fact that it's a black-and-white silent film with Russian subtitles – the best of luck – you'll realise it's basically a crude propaganda film, and like the worst propaganda it's embarrassingly clunky. Again, all the praise is heaped on Eisenstein because no one had made a film before where 'The People' were the heroes. OK, well done, mate, but The People's acting is terrible. The mother who knocks the pram down the Odessa steps in the famous scene dies the most unconvincing death ever; the performances in *Nosferatu* or *Plan 9 From Outer Space* are more believable.

The crude manipulation of emotions in this film completely negates some of the terrific images like the jackboots walking down the steps, the baby in the pram and the ships at anchor in the dawn mist, but even allowing for the clever way these scenes are shot, it's really a collection of animated agitprop posters.

Obviously this is some kind of ambrosia for all those students who spent three years of college in art-house cinemas and then got critics' jobs on *City Limits*, and because *Battleship Potemkin* has the 'correct' politics, it's been allowed to get away with a lot of old tripe.

# *Taxi Driver*

Apart from Bernard Hermann's fantastic music and the opening shot of the New York taxi rolling through the fog, this film consists mostly of De Niro mooching about and mumbling tediously. Then he meets a hooker, shaves his head and starts shooting. Just as it's getting good, it's finished.

# *Singin' in the Rain*

So many films earn their reputation with one show-stopping set piece. To be fair to *Singin' in the Rain* it has two – Gene Kelly's title-song-and-dance routine and Donald O'Connor running up walls singing 'Make 'em Laugh'. But most people forget the terrible bit where Gene gets carried away and inflicts a great big bore of a modern ballet on us for what seems like half the movie. There's plenty of colour in it, as well as Cyd Charisse's amazing legs, but it's like watching a mime artist watching paint dry.

Dear old Gene; he was a fantastic dancer but he got carried away with his 'art' and Hollywood indulged him. His extended ballet scenes like the ones in *Singin' in the Rain* and *An American in Paris* remind me of those terrible episodes of *Starsky and Hutch* when they let David Soul or Paul Michael Glaser direct an episode: you just knew it was all going down the pan after that.

# Lawrence of Arabia
# Gone with the Wind
# The Searchers

● ● ● ● ● ● ● ● ● ● ● ● ● ● ● ● ● ● ● ● ● ● ● ● ● ● ● ● ● ● ● ● ●

Too long, I'm afraid.

# Vertigo

● ● ● ● ● ● ● ● ● ● ● ● ● ● ● ● ● ● ● ● ● ● ● ● ● ● ● ● ● ● ● ● ●

Another overrated film that could have done with half an hour chopped off the running time. James Stewart, a truly fine actor, is reduced to driving around San Francisco, tilting his head to one side and staring at Kim Novak – let's face it, who wouldn't? – but this is supposed to be one of the best films ever, and in the category of psychological thriller, the very best. It's often described by words like 'haunting' and 'atmospheric', which are, as we know, synonyms for 'boring'. Yes, I know it's a film about voyeurism and obsession but couldn't we at least have a decent car chase or something? Another superb soundtrack by Bernard Herrmann, a weird dream sequence and a clever camera trick have elevated this film way above its station. The dream sequence is amazing given the technology available at the time, even though these things are often a gimmick to pad the film out a bit, but *Vertigo* is over two hours long – what it doesn't need is padding! The camera trick, copied by everyone from Spielberg to the makers of breakfast cereal ads, is called a Dolly Zoom or a Trombone Shot, and, to get technical here, is what makes the spiral staircase seem really scary. It's very clever but still just another gimmick.

Aside from the bits of boredom, *Vertigo* has a ludicrous plot with various people running up and down stairs, throwing dummies out of bell towers and a comically bad bit at the end where what looks like an inflatable nun appears from nowhere and frightens someone to death.

Don't worry about me giving the ending away, it'll save you watching the film. Just buy the soundtrack and a copy of the poster and you'll have the best bits.

# *Casablanca*

• • • • • • • • • • • • • • • • • • • • • • • • • • • • • • • • •

I first saw this on a portable black-and-white telly when I was seventeen and thought it was the best film ever. It's never been the same since. Although Humphrey Bogart, Ingrid Bergman and Claude Rains are all magnificent and there's a catchy song at the heart of the story, it suffers from the same sickness that afflicts many very good films, like *Some Like It Hot, Butch Cassidy and the Sundance Kid* and *The Terminator* : overexposure.

Magazine and newspaper polls, endless repeats on TV and, of course, the 'Greatest Ever . . .' list shows have reduced the experience of watching *Casablanca* to a kind of catch-phrase karaoke. Over the years the film has been clipped and quoted for so many different audiences that it only seems to exist as a series of minute-long trailers. So whenever you actually try to watch the whole thing through, you find yourself just waiting for the lines to pop up so you can speak along with them: 'Ah, yes, "A hill of beans in this crazy world". Mm, that bit's good, next it's, "I think this is the beginning of a beautiful friendship"' etc. etc.

Fans of *Casablanca* endlessly quote these lines to people who have never seen the film, which must be intensely annoying for them. It's a bit like those people who always refer to characters in their conversation as if you know exactly who they're talking about.

'Are you out for a drink tonight?'

'Yeah, I'll be in the King's Head at seven-thirty. Dave and Sarah are coming later.'

'Who are they?'

'Dave's one of Andy's mates.'

'Who's Andy?'

'Andy the journalist. He's really funny. You must have met him.'

'No.'

It really is that interesting. In fact, this is a fair representation of any attempt to 'convert' someone to your tastes in anything, be it films, footwear or fish. So it's actually *Casablanca*'s over-quoted dialogue – the very thing that supposedly makes it a 'must see' – that gives you a perfectly good reason not to bother.

# *The Shawshank Redemption*

Like a lot of films that are now 'essential' movies, Shawshank's reputation took a while to grow. It didn't make much impact when it came out, but TV re-runs and DVD sales have catapulted it to the top of loads of movie polls. But why? Again, it's only OK – there are pretty good performances from Morgan 'wise old black guy' Freeman and Tim 'whatever happened to him?' Robbins. It's quite a good story of hope and endurance and someone digs an escape tunnel with a spoon, but there's nothing here to elevate *The Shawshank Redemption* over other prison-flicks like *Birdman of Alcatraz* or *Cool Hand Luke*. What could explain this film's huge popularity with 25-year-old blokes? It's obvious – prison buggery.

Prison dramas are all about drawing the audience into the reality of the 'pen', making them believe it and forcing them to ask themselves if they could survive the horror. In the days when *Cool Hand Luke* was made, the worst you could see cons endure was a bit of trench digging, some cruel guards with sunglasses and the occasional hard-boiled egg eating contest. But in *The Shawshank Redemption* Tim Robbins is cornered by a gang called the Sisters and forced to give blowjobs and bums to some fairly unappealing individuals. That's going to make you want to escape pretty badly, but poor Tim is in the slammer for nineteen years with only his spoon for company – the ultimate young man's nightmare.

I'm not sure a film's reputation should be built on the audience's fear of enforced sodomy, so it's thumbs down for *The Shawshank Redemption*.

# *Pulp Fiction*

• • • • • • • • • • • • • • • • • • • • • • • • • • • • • • • • • • •

This is a collection of sketches and violence from the most overrated director of all time – Quentin Tarantino. You can get a pretty good appreciation of Tarantino's style from his earlier work, *Reservoir Dogs*. It's basically a marketing campaign with some dialogue: a line of blokes in black suits and a cleverly selected soundtrack; the black suits and white shirts clearly inspired by Debbie Harry's backing band and the dialogue by a handful of Barry Levinson films.

*Pulp Fiction* was another collection of suits and guns and rambling trivial dialogue about burgers, chopped up randomly so it looked like 'Tarantino's really messing with the concept of Time here'. He threw in a few more fucks and chucked in a 'soundtrack' of some more records he liked the sound of, although I always thought a soundtrack was something a composer wrote when he'd watched the film. Slapping a bit of old surf music over the opening titles is not film-making, it's what they do in advertising to help you remember brand names. And that's all Tarantino was for a while – a brand name. Buy Tarantino if you want violence, swearing, guns and references to other films that make you feel cool and clever.

Now he's tasted a bit of failure (I'm sure he's down to his last trillion dollars) maybe he will start thinking about making an original film with characters you can care about and a proper story and not just an 'ironic' cast, shooting and stabbing each other in suits.

# *The Empire Strikes Back*

• • • • • • • • • • • • • • • • • • • • • • • • • • • • • • • • • • • • •

Maybe all those *Star Wars* films blur into one for you – various Ewoks and Wookies and Sith and Naboo and other really silly words that sci-fi nerds take so seriously? Well apparently, there is a proper, decent film in among all 37 episodes of the *Star Wars* saga; one, according to fans, that stands above all the others: it's called *The Empire Strikes Back*. This is, in fact, a tacit admission that the others are all actually a bit rubbish and that Part III of the sextet – 'Revenge of the Lord of the Jabba the Dark Side' or something – has got too much CGI; or it's too sentimental, with some really offensively cuddly and cute characters who will never get killed and will always crop up at the end tweeting or bleeping while a couple of humanoids kiss each other and Harrison Ford shakes his head saying, 'You crazy piece of space junk.'

But the real reason why *Star Wars* nerds like *The Empire Strikes*

*Back* so much is that it is absolutely chock-full of Jedi nonsense. Luke Skywalker gets stuck in the snow and then flies off to find Yoda, the wrinkly green ancestor of Gizmo from *Gremlins*, to learn about The Force. When he finds him in a slimy swamp he has to endure about four hours of Jedi gobbledegook from Yoda, which would be hard enough to follow if he wasn't saying all the words in the wrong order: 'Force, Tatooine Vader of the moon Darth is, taught your father the shit yourself you will.'

What actually prevents the *Star Wars* films from achieving greatness is this pseudo-spiritual bunkum, which is all lapped up by the acolytes of The Force as if it were the Sermon on the Mount. These are the kind of people who think it's cool to put 'Jedi' as their religion on the census and it makes it very difficult to enjoy these films for the Robin Hood/Cowboys and Indians/Flash Gordon romps that they really are, knowing that the nerds have added all of this to their repertoire of *Star Wars* catch-phrase karaoke. All together now: 'These aren't the droids you're looking for. The force is strong in this one. Obi-Wan has taught you well. No, Luke, I Am Your Father.'

# ART

Believe it or not there's a book out called *1001 Paintings You Must See Before You Die*. Well, they're all in the book, so why not just buy it and have a look? Job done.

# BOOKS

However snooty and snobby people can be over their taste in films and music, they can never cause as much harm as the literary snob.

Film buffs, however much they claim to be 'cineastes', can always fall for a *Toy Story* or a *Gladiator* like the rest of us: a good film is a great leveller. Musical snobs, be they lovers of 'serious music' ('classical music' to most people) or art-rock or jazz, can only ruin so much of your life with their 'must hear' recommendations. You're not really going to sit through an entire Joni Mitchell album if you find her high-pitched warbling offensive; you'll give her ten minutes, tops. Even if you forced yourself to listen to an entire symphony by Gorecki, it's going to take up no more than an hour of your time.

But recommended lists of 'essential' reading are the most

pernicious of all. Lists of physical achievements or magical holiday destinations or wonderful restaurants or fabulous hotels make you feel like your life has been wasted; a list of great books you should have read makes you feel like your *brain* has been wasted. It's somehow far more offensive and likely to spur you to action. You can turn Nirvana's *Nevermind* off after Track 1 because the rest of it is mostly rubbish, but somehow books force you to plod on. Most people embarking on a journey into a new book will feel they have to hack through a hundred pages of dense undergrowth before their conscience will allow them to give it up as a lost cause. But how many people feel secure enough in their own judgement even to do that? How many times have we all ploughed on to the end to find there's actually no treasure after all? A book, even a useless one, can take several days out of your life, so it's a big investment.

Of course, there will always be newspaper and magazine features about how to bluff your way through certain major authors and their novels, like *Brodie's Notes* for grown-ups, but we must reject that kind of thing. It's playing the literary snobs' game; a bit like wearing fake fur – you're not killing the animal but you're admitting that its dead skin makes you look good.

The best way to fight the massed ranks of recommended books is with an offensively glib and, if possible, ill-informed reason for not bothering with them.

# *War and Peace*

· · · · · · · · · · · · · · · · · · · · · · · · · · · · · · · · ·

Way, way too long.

# *Crime and Punishment*

· · · · · · · · · · · · · · · · · · · · · · · · · · · · · · · · ·

First fifty pages too depressing.

# *The Iliad and The Odyssey*

● ● ● ● ● ● ● ● ● ● ● ● ● ● ● ● ● ● ● ● ● ● ● ● ● ● ● ● ● ● ● ● ● ● ● ● ● ●

Unfortunately I can't dismiss these out of hand as I was once forced to read them (no one in their right mind would do so for pleasure), so I'll have to do it based on experience. The *Iliad* is one of the most boring books ever written and it's not just a boring book, it's a boring epic poem; all repetitive battle scenes with a lot of reproaching and challenging and utterances escaping the barrier of one's teeth and nostrils filling with dirt and helmet plumes nodding menacingly. There's a big fight between Achilles and Hector and that's about it.

The *Odyssey* is a bit better because at least it's a journey with some monsters and witches and whirlpools and stuff, but to be honest it's nowhere near as good as the film of *Jason and the Argonauts* or *Sinbad the Sailor*. The very idea that you are somehow culturally incomplete without knowledge of Homer is ridiculous. He didn't come up with 'Is this the face that launched a thousand ships?' – that was Christopher Marlowe a few thousand years later. Nor did he bother to write about the Wooden Horse – that's in Virgil's Latin epic, the *Aeneid*, which also contains the only famous quote anyone can remember about the Trojan War– 'I fear Greeks bearing gifts'. Better to fear Greeks writing epic poems.

# *Freakonomics*
# *The Tipping Point*
# *The Beauty Myth*

● ● ● ● ● ● ● ● ● ● ● ● ● ● ● ● ● ● ● ● ● ● ● ● ● ● ● ● ● ● ● ● ●

Beware the populist academic tome. America's bookshops are awash with them. *Freakonomics* is one of the recent biggies, and it's a good read – I wouldn't say brilliant. It has one or two fascinating studies in it but like all economics, it's not rocket science, or any kind of science (that really winds economists up), but the way America reacted to it, you'd think the authors had invented binary numbers. James Gleick wrote a popular book called *Faster* – it's about how the pace of life is speeding up and we are so busy these days we don't have time to relax. Really, you amaze me?

Remarkably, this kind of book is starting to crop up on 'essential' lists in the UK, because they are supposed to have changed the way we think or made us look at the world in a different way.

I don't know if Gladwell and Wolf are genuine academics – I couldn't be arsed to Google them – if they are, they are probably Emeritus Professors of the bleeding obvious.

Naomi Wolf's book, *The Beauty Myth*, is about how women feel under pressure to look good and lose weight. There you go. That's it. I could get a similarly sophisticated level of socio-political analysis from the fishwives on *Loose Women*.

Naomi so clearly had her finger on the pulse of Western women and Americans in particular, that she was hired by Al Gore to fight his disastrous election campaign against Bush in 2000. She advised him to be a bit more manly and wear earth tones and he lost to a man whose idea of fun is throwing horseshoes at a stick.

Malcolm Gladwell's *The Tipping Point* is about things reaching a point where they 'tip' from one condition to another, like a see-saw or a disease or something. That's about the whole book in a nutshell; some things are unpopular, then they are culty for a bit, then they are really popular and there was a point at which they 'tipped' from being culty to really popular. Can't fault the logic there, but it's hardly the Theory of Evolution, is it?

Gladwell tells some stories about things like Hush Puppies, which no one wore until some people did and then lots of them did and – ta-da! That'll be several million dollars and a reputation as one of the world's foremost thinkers, please. There's some mildly interesting stuff in the book about how *Sesame Street* was made and how the American Revolution started, but there is no great insight here – it's all post-rationalising and hindsight. There is absolutely no practical application for whatever he thinks a Tipping Point is. I'd love to see some explanation of how on earth this book 'tipped' from being a journalist's extended think-piece into an international bestseller, and how the phrase 'tipping point' has come to be routinely used by news reporters on every single story, from Iraqi insurgents to summer flooding. It's almost as if journalists are waiting for the next 'zeitgeisty' phrase to drop into their mental inbox. At the moment it's 'any time soon', which has suddenly and annoyingly sprung up in English journalism as another way of saying 'in the near future'.

Maybe Gladwell is actually taking the piss out of everyone and has succeeded in creating a bestseller phenomenon by writing about bestselling phenomena. He also wrote another hugely successful book called *Blink* about – I'm not making this up – trusting your instinct and making snap judgements. I'm not sure how many pages he managed to spin that one out for, but my snap judgement is Malcolm Gladwell's taking money for old rope.

# *Fear and Loathing in Las Vegas*

Dreary ramblings of a unreliable and workshy tosspot. Its sole distinction consists in the creation of 'Gonzo journalism', which made it OK for journalists, particularly rock journalists, to get shit-faced with whoever they happened to be writing about.

# Animal Farm

It's such an obvious allegory I don't know why Orwell bothered. Napoleon the pig is Stalin? Oh, so I'll just read a history book about Stalin and the corruption of the Communist ideal, then.

# The Catcher in the Rye

It's just about OK. Most people who have heard of it know it drove that nutter to shoot John Lennon. Holden Caulfield is really quite annoying and could have done with a spell in the army.

# Catch 22

One of the number books, along with *Slaughterhouse 5*, that sound cool. The film's better – you can figure out what's going on.

# *The Dice Man*

It's entertaining for a hundred pages but by then you've seen all there is to see, so you can pack it in with a clear conscience. Basically, this fairly unpleasant bloke does whatever his dice tell him to do, which is often quite terrible. But there's a flaw in the structure of this book. He writes down an option for each number of the dice and then lets the dice decide what he should do. 'Throw a six and rape the woman upstairs'?! How did that get on his list of things to do? If he'd written down, 'Throw a six and put some more mastic around the shower tray' or 'Throw a six and have *three* crispy pancakes for tea' he wouldn't have got into so much trouble. 'Oh, but I must obey the dice – they decide my fate!' Well put some other bloody stuff on the dice, then!

*The Dice Man* is known as a 'High Concept' book and is still very much in vogue as a genre – there's another one called *Yes Man* – where author Danny Wallace says yes to every opportunity to see where that leads him. What a ludicrous idea and extremely dangerous; anyone who followed that advice would be the Anti-me. I'm sure if we ever met, the universe would explode.

# Jane Eyre, Pride and Prejudice and stuff like that

I haven't read any of these books because from what I can gather it's Mills and Boon from the olden days, and really boring Mills and Boon at that. I did try reading a Jane Austen novel once, but it hadn't got going by fifty pages so I guiltily gave up; the characters spoke in a very oblique way and it seemed to be all about hypocrisy and manners and convention; worse than that, it was really difficult to find the doing word in a sentence and that, I'm afraid, is the problem with a lot of these books.

I will be honest and admit I'm lumping a century of fiction together because whenever the adaptations appear on television in some shape or form, they all seem to look the same – carriages drive up to big houses carrying very contemporary totty in period costume with a sizeable proportion of knocker on show. Defenders of romantic fiction will argue that the costumes are irrelevant to the times they were written in and if they had been dramatised in their time, I would not have noticed the costumes. They might also argue that I wouldn't dismiss

*EastEnders* or *Coronation Street* or *Silent Witness* or *Prime Suspect* or *Mistresses* because people are wearing the same clothes. But you know what? I bloody do. They are all, to a large extent, the same. Kay Mellor, Lynda La Plante, Debbie Horsfield and all the soap writers produce narratives and characters which grip their audience because they recognise them and the situations they're in and they know where the author's going with the story. That's why these writers are so successful – broadcasters know what they are going to deliver, and that, to be blunt, is TV for the ladies and not me.

# À la Recherche du Temps Perdu

Yes, yes, Proust tasted a biscuit that made him think of childhood, we've all done that. If I want to remember my childhood I look at some photographs.

# *Great Expectations*

● ● ● ● ● ● ● ● ● ● ● ● ● ● ● ● ● ● ● ● ● ● ● ● ● ● ● ● ● ● ● ● ●

I actually love Charles Dickens – a warm-hearted lover of humanity, railing passionately against injustice. But I think he's better on the telly. I can imagine someone who has never read Dickens reaching for the nearest bargepole at the mention of his name. If you know anything of him it'll be from *Oliver!* or *A Christmas Carol*, but you'll be disappointed to find out that his other books, e.g. *Great Expectations* have no songs in them, least of all loveable cockney sing-along songs; nor do they have anything like the excellent time-travelling ghosts and apparitions lugging great chains forged in hell from their own sins that you find in *A Christmas Carol*. Basically, most of Dickens' novels seem to have just too many words and too many characters, all with silly names like Mrs Fozzycog and Unglebert Tickswitch.

# For Whom the Bell Tolls

• • • • • • • • • • • • • • • • • • • • • • • • • • • • • • • • •

The Hemingway style is impressive at first. Simple sentences with few descriptions. He avoids adverbs and adjectives and, as a change from the over-elaborate works of Dickens and Austen, it's OK for a while. Then you realise it's a bit dry and boring and the more you find out about Hemingway, the more you realise he was a bore too: a terrible macho bore obsessed with bullfighting, guns, boxing and trying to catch big fish; really quite a tiresome bloke you wouldn't want to spend time with. *For Whom the Bell Tolls* is about the Spanish Civil War, which he witnessed as a journalist. There is a lot of shooting and moodiness. OK, so he went to report on a bloody civil war as a journalist and found it disturbing and it affected him very deeply – how's that for an original insight? I believe Feargal Keane, Martin Bell and Kate Adie and about a hundred other foreign correspondents had a similar experience; I'll bet their books use adjectives. Probably the most overrated author of all time.

# *Ulysses*

There's a brilliant scene in the much-underrated sitcom *It Ain't Half Hot, Mum*, when Sergeant Major Williams (Windsor Davies) snatches a book from Mr La-di-dah Gunner Graham and says:

'What's this you're reading? Useless?'

'*Ulysses*, Sergeant Major.'

Even though the Sergeant Major is the villain of the show, we can't help sympathising with his view of James Joyce, because Mr La-di-dah Gunner Graham is a bit of a tit. Even a mainstream 1970s sitcom audience knew that *Ulysses* is a pretentious book, notoriously difficult to read.

At school I remember my English teacher saying that he knew no one who had managed to get to the end of it. It does sound rubbish, doesn't it? I'd have thought it was the duty of a great book to drag you along to the last page. But in a way, that's good to know: if it's famously hard going you have the perfect excuse not to bother with it.

# *Lord of the Rings*

The best I can say about this book is that it was a very useful tool at school for helping to choose your friends. Carrying a copy of Tolkien's monstrous tome was the equivalent of a leper's bell: 'Unclean! Unclean!' I knew I would have nothing in common with anyone who had read it. Their taste in music, clothes, television, everything, was predetermined by their devotion to Gandalf. Without a shadow of a doubt, in a few years these people would be going to Peter Gabriel gigs and reading *Dune*.

But now, three decades and three blockbuster movies later, the handbook for all sci-fi nerds, prog rockers and war-gamers is acceptable reading material for millions, and responsible grown-ups take their children to see it. You can bet the makers of *Dungeons and Dragons*, *Dr Who* and *Hitchhiker's Guide to the Galaxy* sank to their knees with relief that they could crank up the hobgoblin/elf/dwarf/jelly-faced-green-monster merchandise machine once again; while the rest of us felt like some hideous beast had been brought back from the dead.

# ENOUGH CULTURE...

It's time to go back to some of the slightly more bizarre but absolutely genuine ambitions that some nutters out there think are worth acheiving before you cash in your chips at the Big Casino.

# Make Friends with a Famous Person

Why on earth would anyone want to do this? Granted, lots of famous people are fantastically wealthy and many are quite generous with it, but you only have to flick through a couple of star biographies to see that it's the friends and family who are on the receiving end when the Star lashes out.

Let's leave to one side for the moment the practicalities of making friends with a famous person: how you select your target; orchestrate a meeting; keep them talking beyond a couple of sentences as they are likely to think you are a weirdo stalker – what are you actually going to talk about? Maybe you could get a job building their swimming pool and strike up a conversation about chlorine filters, or fake a fascination for their pet subject (which in some cases, so I've heard, is porn). Let's assume you've gone to these ridiculous lengths already, and got away with it, what does hanging out with a famous person involve?

It's *de rigueur* for them to be hassled by people (like you, for starters). They get hassled because the thing they are famous for takes them into someone else's life; other people think they know them. This is a common complaint from famous people – complete strangers feel it's OK to shout things at them in the street or comment on their personal appearance. Ask Wogan about that, but get to know him first, obviously.

There is an inoffensive way to encounter a celeb in the street – the Celebrity Handshake (not to be confused with 'six degrees of separation', that's not even a contest: just shake hands with the Queen, she's met everyone – game over). The American author Garrison Keillor tells you how to do this in *We Are Still Married*. You smile at your chosen celeb, extend your hand and say, 'I really like your work'. Who could possibly take exception to that? Unless it was someone like James Blunt and it couldn't possibly be true: you'd have to be taking the piss.

Suppose you get past the handshake stage. The first thing the famous person wants to know is, 'What does this person want from me?' People who talk to famous people usually want something, say an autograph or a photograph to prove they are who they say they are or, worse, proof that they can really do what they do for a living – be funny, do some acting, sing now, fall over, do the face, say the catchphrase (Ricky Gervais deals with this brilliantly in *Extras*). This is often accompanied by poking or jovial shoving or some other form of manhandling – 'Stand there for the photograph', 'Ooh, you're fatter than I thought' etc. It's so difficult to engage with a famous person if they don't already know you and they have no professional reason to be involved with you, because they will always expect you to be after a piece of them.

If famous people have any true friends at all, they'll be people from way back. So here's a tip: make friends with someone *before* they're famous. You know that eccentric kid in the corner? The one who makes the weird noises under his breath and acts a bit Tourettes-y, or the one who writes the imaginative stories, the one who can dance, the one who always volunteers for school productions, the really good singer – well, make friends with them. Don't join in with everyone else who ridicules them or shoves them in the dinner queue or sends them foul text messages or gives them Chinese burns; instead, be their mate; hedge your bets, be as nice to as many people as possible, then maybe they'll stay friends with you no matter how famous they are. And if they don't you can always sell your story to the papers.

# Try Drugs

People won't believe it if you say you've never tried drugs. 'Oh, come on, you must have! How can you talk about something if you haven't tried it?' It's this you-have-to-try-it-once attitude that really winds me up.

'It's better to regret doing something than regret never doing it.' Oh really? Tell that to the man in the Parexel drugs trials with a head the size of an elephant. Admittedly that's not what most people mean by drugs, although every time you ingest an illegal chemical substance you're trusting an irresponsible arse-hole you don't know with your mental health. Cocaine, heroin, cannabis, E, they all rely on dealers – the kind of people who take Harry Lyme from *The Third Man* as their role model. To them, you are an ant with a wallet.

Of course, there are some great new drugs you can make or grow yourself, like crack and skunk. Not only is the drug more potent, but you can rest assured it hasn't been adulterated with rat poison, toilet cleaner and cement – unless you stash it in the cupboard under my sink.

I'll admit I'm frightened of taking drugs because I'm pretty weak-willed and wouldn't trust myself not to lose control. Who knows where it could end up? Drug fans insist that illegal substances open up a whole world of new experiences – deep relaxation, a sense of wellbeing, of an endless great big hug, feelings of invincibility and ecstasy. That's as maybe, but there's also paranoia, schizophrenia, domestic violence, kleptomania, prostitution and sucking off a Turkish businessman in a phone box for money. My risk-management model requires me happily to forego the ecstasy and wellbeing so as to avoid the possibility of fellating said Levantine merchant.

Drug devotees like to cite alcohol as a much more dangerous drug than any illegal substance. Yes, alcohol is a drug and yes, it's terrible and yes, thousands die and yes, it causes more marital break-up and criminal activity and boring anecdotes than anything else, but let's face it, we can't get rid of alcohol. It's too late. The gin is out of the bottle. Anyway, it's not a question of drugs *or* alcohol, it's drugs *and* alcohol. Whatever recreational substances you might fancy, they will always be in addition to alcohol. I wonder how people who campaign for alcohol and cannabis to have the same legal status would respond to a government who said, 'OK, you know what? You're right about alcohol – it is as bad as cannabis. We'll ban that too.' The truth is (and this is highly appropriate, given the title of this book) it's just too much trouble to try and abolish alcohol; at least with drugs there's still a chance to do something about it.

So far, my only argument against drugs has been that I am personally too scared to take them, and I don't think that will cut much ice with the majority of users, so I am going to make a more serious appeal – an appeal that really addresses the fundamentals. Think of the cost. Seriously, think of how much it will cost you in pounds to have a drug habit, bearing in mind that you're unlikely to cut back on your alcohol consumption and, depending on your drug of choice, you're equally unlikely to cut down on food. So, how much extra are your drugs going to cost you every week? Forty or fifty quid? That's two and a half grand a year. Now I ask you – is feeling brilliant for two hours a week really worth more to you than two and a half grand a year? You could have a really nice holiday somewhere like the Isle of Wight for that. I'm right, aren't I?

# Get a Tattoo

What does a tattoo say about you? That you're a bit rebellious, a little bit daring? That you're an individual and you choose to use your body as a means of expressing yourself? Or that you're stuck with a stupid doodle on your backside for the rest of your life, which you can never get rid of properly? We all know a story about a bloke dumped by his girlfriend the day after he'd tattooed her name on his arm, and the one about the fan of Olympic gold-medallist Kelly Holmes, who turned up to welcome her back to Britain with the name 'Kelly Homes' on her back. But every tattoo will come to embarrass its owner one day.

And if it doesn't, it should.

The six-year-old son of a friend of mine asked him why people have tattoos and my friend said, 'Because they have no class'. His son has a good memory and a loud voice, which has led to some embarrassment in the queue at the Kentucky Fried Chicken, but never was a truer word spoken. It's impossible to have class *and* a tattoo. Those nice girls who, for some bizarre reason, think it's attractive to have some kind of Celtic symbol or butterfly or heraldic device on their back poking up above their pants should be aware of the slang term for these tattoos – a 'tramp stamp' or a 'slag tag'. They're a bit like cigarettes, which can transform any pretty girl into a reincarnation of Hilda Ogden or Yootha Joyce. Amy Winehouse is always photographed with tattoos and fags, lending her all the charm and allure of a Holloway Prison drugs mule.

David Beckham – by anyone's reckoning a handsome man – has had so many tattoos he's running out of body space. Recently he has had some angel-themed nonsense needled on to the back of his neck, and he now reminds me of one of those meatheads guarding the villain's hideout, who usually get bumped off in the first reel of a James Bond film.

This isn't the worst of Beckham's tattoo crimes, however. He has a tattoo on his arm of his wife's name in Hindi. Apparently it's less tacky than having it done in English. Maybe, but only if you spell it right, which he didn't. All over the world people are having Hindi and Sanskrit and Chinese and Japanese symbols etched into their skin without the faintest idea of what they say. A bloke in a dingy parlour with a needle and some ink says he's tattooing 'Shining Star' or 'I love my mum' on your arm in Kanji, but he could be writing

'Chicken Katsu Curry with Tempura Vegetables' for all you know. Why do people think 'expressing' themselves in a mystical, Eastern language is more sophisticated than doing so in their own language? The answer often given is quite revealing: 'It's something I understand but others don't necessarily know the meaning of.' Or put another way – it would be just plain embarrassing to have an inspirational slogan like 'Never give up' or 'Fount of wisdom' written on your backside in English.

Tattoos signify many different things in different cultures, but one of their universal functions is as a symbol of ownership. A tattoo is a step up from being branded as a slave. Like the 'yoot' of today who wear low-slung trousers to emulate prisoners – who are forced to dress like that so they can't run very fast – people who sport tattoos aren't what you might call 'aiming high'. It seems a very odd way to express your individuality.

# Go to Glastonbury (or any other rock festival)

● ● ● ● ● ● ● ● ● ● ● ● ● ● ● ● ● ● ● ● ● ● ● ● ● ● ● ● ● ● ● ● ● ●

This is now an obligatory rite of passage for all cool, happening, with-it, switched-on, sorted, sussed, . . . er, buff(?) teenagers. What self-respecting parent would dream of obstructing their barely pubescent child's pilgrimage to the shrine of Glastonbury, Reading or that park where the 'T' is?

When I was seventeen all the cool, adventurous kids in my sixth form went to Knebworth to see Led Zeppelin, leaving all the jerks, nerds, geeks, wallflowers and swots behind. If you drew a Venn diagram of my sixth form, I would intersect with all of those subsets, so I was one of those clinging to my coffee mug back in the common room, praying for it to piss down.

In our hearts one or two of us knew that, despite the outside chance of seeing Jacqueline Stebbings (my heart's desire) half-naked in a tent, we were right not to go. This was 1979 – surely everyone had heard the Undertones by now and thrown away their Pink Floyd and Yes albums, as we had? Well, it may have been 1979, but it was also Yorkshire, and punk or 'New Wave', as everyone called it then, was not to make landfall until about

1981. So the scaly dinosaur tails of folk rock, prog rock, stadium rock and cock rock were still swishing dangerously. If you pointed out that guitar solos were musical masturbation and flares and long hair were for hippy twats, you would be howled down and your heroes, Fergal Sharkey and Pete Shelley, would be derided as ugly, spotty wimps who couldn't play their instruments.

So the cool thing to do was to gather up a kagoul, a tent and a sleeping bag – enough nylon to wrap up the whole of Hertfordshire like Christo – and head off to Knebworth to see 'the Zepp', supported by Southside Johnny and the Asbury Jukes, Fairport Convention and, God help us, Todd Rundgren.

I have nurtured a pathological hatred of rock festivals ever since. And now, almost thirty years later, more than the memory of that missed opportunity to see Jacqueline Stebbings half-naked, it's the hideous hinterland of the outdoor gig that really gets up my pipe.

For starters, tents are utterly vile: apart from when you're a kid and the tent is in your back garden and you know you are only five yards from a civilised wee, electricity and pop. Tents also flap and billow in the wind like crazy, so it's impossible to sleep, they leak, they are freezing and they stink of . . . of *tent* stink. People always light camp fires (I really hate that), everyone wants a piss at the same time as you, total gits walk about on stilts or juggle wearing those jester hats with the pointy bits, white rastas are always trying to sell you beanburgers and there is always, always, at every single performance at every outdoor gig ever, the same annoying girl, perched on some bloke's shoulders at the front, swaying and ululating like a mourner at an Iraqi funeral, and blocking your bloody view.

Or so I'm told. I've never actually been to a proper one. I did stand far too close to a terrible Anti-Apartheid gig on Clapham Common in 1985. It was famous for Boy George dowsing himself in Homepride flour for some reason no one can remember – maybe he thought it was heroin? I only lived two miles away and I was homesick.

Happily, Knebworth '79 was a critical and financial disaster for Led Zeppelin, but our sixth-form avant-garde had got the taste and they went on to Glastonbury a few months later, where Michael Eavis was trying to recreate the train wreck of his late 60s festivals. They drummed up the likes of Peter Gabriel, John Martyn and Steve Hillage to peddle their self-indulgent wares, but what was this further down the bill? Tom Robinson? Surely not Tom '2-4-6-8 Motorway' Robinson? The Only Ones? The 'Another Girl Another Planet' Only Ones? The UK Subs? The 'actually quite shit but still a punk band' UK Subs? Why were they damaging their credibility by sharing a stage with Genesis hobgoblin Peter Gabriel? Still, no worries; Glastonbury '79 was a flop too, and rock festivals disappeared from the radar for a few years.

Then something bad happened. Far more disturbing than The Only Ones appearing on the same bill as Steve Hillage. Bands I really loved and singer/songwriters I admired and respected started playing there. The Smiths!? Elvis Costello!? People I liked started going and saying what a wonderful 'happening' experience it was. Magazines and newspapers I thought were intelligent began writing about Glastonbury, and not to suggest the whole site be rotovated and salt ploughed into the fields.

I blame John Peel for all this, with his damned broad-mindedness and musical eclecticism and his annual family outing to the tented village. He made it acceptable for middle-class parents, and not just New Age Crusties, to carry their infants in papooses through mud like Passchendaele, smiling at drug dealers as they squelched their way to the knitted yoghurt concession. Soon all the Millies and Archies were mixing with the Moonbeams and Hazelnuts, until the mid-90s, by which time Oasis were playing at Knebworth to the biggest crowd of idiots ever assembled outdoors. By then, the corporate sponsors had arrived at Glastonbury, along with the hundred-quid ticket; the BBC had also pitched camp, piping the 'counter culture' into a million living rooms, while BBC execs wooed top TV talent in luscious hospitality tents with my bloody licence money.

The die-hard festival-going flower-children are as disgruntled about this as I am, but for different reasons. They see the integrity of their agrarian love-in being compromised by Babylon, Mammon, The Man, or whatever they call capitalism these days. I, on the other hand, see some people I might have had a drink with in normal circumstances playing at hippies in a field for the weekend, like they were in some freaky tie-dyed Territorial Army.

If you really want to undergo a rite of passage where you spend a few nights away from home with some friends in a tent, join the venture scouts.

If you want to see Amy Winehouse or Arctic Monkeys live, go to a venue with walls and a roof. If you want to hear them at their best, buy a CD (it's miles better than live music anyway). But if you want to say you've 'been there' in a field with 100,000 other tossers, go to Glastonbury.

# Have a Meaningful Conversation with a Beggar

On the face of it, this is a perfectly laudable ambition. What could possibly be the problem with something so clearly altruistic? Well, the problem lies with the word 'meaningful'. All those lists of things to do before you die are compiled out of pretty much undiluted selfishness. They are all about you and how much you can get out of life before you snuff it. Just like 'Look into a Child's Eyes, See Yourself and Smile' and 'Visit Auschwitz and Vow Never to Forget', this is one of those 'life-changing experiences' which is totally self-centred.

Let's leave aside the fact that it's becoming increasingly difficult to have a meaningful conversation with a beggar if you don't speak Romanian, and look at the objective behind this 'meaningful conversation' – it's not going to be very meaningful for the beggar, is it? After you've moved on to your tryst at the All Bar One, they're not going to say to themselves: 'Well, that *was* an excellent conversation; I'll look at the films of Werner Herzog in a different light.' It will be a meaningful conversation for the beggar if it ends with you saying: 'So lovely to have met you, here are the keys to my house', or 'Cheers, mate, here's fifty quid'.

There's bugger-all chance of that happening, so whatever 'meaning' there might be in this 'meaningful' conversation is going to be coming to the chatterer, not the chattee, and I'm sure it's supposed to be something like this: 'Oh, he had such an interesting story to tell', or 'Oh, he was such a wise old man', or 'Oh, she was such an interesting and educated young lady' or 'Oh, he had built such an ingenious cardboard house'. Well, terrific, I hope that makes you feel better. If someone could walk away from a conversation with a beggar thinking, 'Oh, how lucky I am not to be in that situation' they might well have discovered something quite meaningful, but unless they can translate this into handing over some cash at the end of it, then it would be just as pointless and patronising as any of the other outcomes. The immediate requirement of a beggar is not the pleasure of your company, but money. That's why they sit where they sit.

'But surely,' you'll say, 'they'll only spend it on drink, or drugs?' – and what would you spend it on? Clarinet lessons?

There is something undeniably good at the heart of people who are prepared to stop and talk to the homeless, but you'll probably find that those who are doing it out of sincere motives and not for the chance of a 'meaningful conversation', are doing it on a regular basis and all the time. They will probably help to run soup kitchens and work in hostels and church halls and give up their entire Christmas to help other people. You can't just dip a toe into social work. You can't have a guilt-assuaging chat for ten minutes and say, 'Been there, done that, bought the *Big Issue*.'

Do I practice what I'm preaching? No, of course not, and to diffuse the slight whiff of sanctimony in this item, I'll throw in a slightly cruel but quite funny homeless-person joke.

There's a man outside a pub who's accosted by a homeless person: 'If I tell you a joke and you laugh, will you give me a pound?'

'OK,' said the drinker, 'but if your joke is no good and I tell a joke that makes *you* laugh, you give me a pound.' The homeless man agreed and told a weak joke that fell flat. So it was the drinker's turn and he said to the homeless man:

'Knock knock.'

'Who's there?'

'Hang on, you said you were homeless!'

# Make Yourself Spend a Day in Auschwitz and Vow Never to Forget

I have seen this appear on more than one wish list and I'm still trying to fathom the thinking behind this one. Would you be

RICHARD WILSON

incapable of remembering the Holocaust if you didn't make yourself spend half a day in Auschwitz? Or is it that you could only have the experience of 'vowing never to forget' in the authentic concentration camp setting? There's an underlying self-centredness in this ambition I'm finding hard to pin down, maybe because I still can't believe this is on anyone's check list in the first place.

The unpalatable truth is we *always* forget, those of us who were lucky enough not to be directly affected. Life goes on and the important things are forgotten as soon as we notice a crack in the ceiling or one of our kids has a verruca. We need to be brought up short by a good piece of writing or television, or a shocking event.

Driving through France a few years ago, I came across a town called Oradour-sur-Glane. The name rang a bell and I remembered it was featured in the opening sequence of the brilliant documentary series *The World At War*. It's the town the Nazis destroyed in 1944, just because it happened to be in their way. Everyone in the town was murdered and the French have preserved it just as the Nazis left it, so that no one would forget. But I had forgotten until I happened across it that day. It would not have been right for me to have deliberately visited this place, knowing what it was, in order to be intentionally shocked by it. If you are going to visit a concentration camp for the purpose of 'making a vow', you already know all you need to know and you're indulging in nothing more than grief tourism.

# Build a Tree House

If you look at enough lists of things to do before you die you begin to notice a pattern. Among all the daredevilry of bungee jumping and skydiving and the unforgettable travel destinations is a yearning to go back to nature or childhood or something more primitive and supposedly more 'honest' than whatever you're doing with your life now.

Building a tree house is a classic attempt to regain lost childhood. Ah, those innocent days of skinned knees! Tin boxes full of secrets, a tyre on the end of a rope, dangerous woodland fires and stolen porn mags.

For Americans in particular, the tree house is a rather pathetic symbol of the yuppy's attempt to escape from the rat race; to experience something authentic and genuine. It's all a bit obvious, though, isn't it? Let's get back to nature by, durr, living in trees.

A big fan of this simplistic life is Naomi Wolf (see 'Books'). She became an overnight literary sensation with her very first book. But then after her great success, she started to feel a bit stressed out; she was, like, totally a slave to her publishers and her laptop and her mobile and shit? So to 'rediscover herself' she went off to build a tree house, as anyone would, with her poet/philosopher dad.

And guess what? By sawing up wood she got back to nature and began to discover life's true meaning, as well as write another book about it: 'When people spend time around my dad, they are always quitting their sensible jobs with good benefits to become schoolteachers, or agitators, or lutenists.' (*The Treehouse: Eccentric Wisdom from My Father on How to Live, Love, and See.*)

But I'm sure you don't all have philosopher/poet fathers who can chop wood and use an adze, so what are the chances of you successfully pulling off the self-build tree house? Let's be honest, none at all. The best any of us could manage is a wonky platform with a ladder.

Robinson Crusoe did manage to build a brilliant tree house; at least he did on the telly when I was a kid. It was an amazing fortress, with high walls made out of sharpened tree trunks, an observation platform, kitchen, a place for his dog and a veranda for his slave to sleep on. But he had bugger all else to do and it took him 28 years. You might want to do it faster than that. Well you can, by paying a hundred grand to treeadventures.co.uk. Seriously, they will take your specifications, build the thing in your garden for you and connect up all the electricity and water and outdoor heaters you want. Yes, the carefree days of childhood can be yours again if your City bonus has just kicked in.

So you sit in your tree house and then do what? Well, if the elfin dribbling on tree-house-based Internet chat rooms is any guide, you could hang out with these people

> GELFLING: 'I was talking to Keri on msn and she said something about having our own treehouse and that is such a kickass thought.'
> MAIDEN: 'Yeah I really want one. We would have colorful comfy pillows to sit on, lots of incense to burn, crayons to paint, tea afternoons.'
> GELFLING: 'I have always dreamt of living in a huge tree in a dark forest with elves you know like in Lord Of The Rings?'

Doesn't that sound brilliant? I'll bet right now dozens of you are on your way to B&Q to buy the wood and nails.

# Build an Igloo

For survivalists, hippies and general outdoor types, the igloo is also something natural and therefore obviously better than anything man-made like a nylon tent. You can find loads of websites devoted to the construction of igloos and I'm quoting honestly from one of them:

'Building an igloo is easy and fun; much warmer than a tent and can be built just about anywhere. It will take between three and six hours.'

I don't know where to begin with that statement.

*'Warmer than a tent'*? Yeah, maybe, but not warm enough for me. I bet my house with the heating on full is miles warmer.

*'Can be built just about anywhere'*? Right, anywhere there is at least a metre's depth of snow so hard that you have to cut it with a special snow saw. My, it's so convenient, it's like setting up a deckchair.

But here's the killer:

*'Building an igloo is easy and fun . . . it will take between three and six hours.'* Well, somebody stop me! I'm putting on my thermals right now. I can't believe people aren't building igloos all the time! Six hours in subzero temperatures cutting up snow with a saw? While the other guy with the nylon tent has not only erected it, he's cooked a three-course meal, had a good night's

sleep and got up again for breakfast. The only person I've ever seen comfortable in an igloo is Pingu.

Building a teepee (also, obviously, much better than a nylon tent) is pretty much the same kind of back-breaking labour involving a dozen or so thirteen-foot poles and three miles of canvas. Don't forget to include smoke flaps and all joins must be hand stitched – oh, dear, it's raining.

People don't need to live in tents, there are houses and flats purpose-built for living in. Camping has never appealed to me apart from the cheapness – I like that about it – and you can do it in England, but if you must make things difficult for yourself by living where there's no running water or electricity, why make the process of tent building so laborious? Even the Native Americans don't bother to live in tents these days.

The TV presenter Bear Grylls is the kind of person who loves building tents out of canvas or houses out of snow, or beds out of stoat droppings but only because he can make money out of it through TV shows that dreamy fantasists will watch. And Bear Grylls isn't stupid; he doesn't stay in the tent – after a day's filming he goes back to a hotel.

By building stuff like igloos and teepees you are supposed to become more like those deeply spiritual and wise people who used to live in them and whom the white, liberal middle classes, exploited years before we were born. The telltale sign of the aspiring Arapaho or wannabe Wappinger, who would perhaps rather be running with wolves on a hillside than running a family saloon, is the Dreamcatcher in the bedroom. So let's add this to the list…

# 84

# Make A Dreamcatcher

Dreamcatchers are supposed to have been used by Native Americans as a way of keeping evil spirits and bad luck at bay. You hang a hoop with a net across it in your wigwam, teepee or wikiup and during the night it catches bad dreams in the net, which are destroyed by the morning sunlight, a bit like Dracula. As a bonus, it allows good dreams to slip through into your head,

bringing great happiness and making it the most remarkable invention since the television; why aren't Sony interested in this?

There are literally hundreds of websites which offer instructions on how to make your own dreamcatcher, often as a helpful aid to teaching kids about other cultures; schoolchildren are encouraged to hang a dreamcatcher over their bed to catch the bad dreams and ensure an undisturbed night's sleep. There's probably one out there especially for teenage boys called a wetdreamcatcher. You have to feel sorry for the Native Americans, many of whom used to treasure the traditional dreamcatcher as a symbol of tribal unity, because a lot of the ones you can make yourself or buy in New Age wind-chime shops are really, insultingly tacky. The legend of the dreamcatcher is that a god in the form of a spider wove a web around a tribesman's willow hoop. The spider told him the web would catch bad dreams and the good ones would find their way through the hole in the middle. Some of the most absurd and tatty interpretations from the world of pic'n'mix spirituality have the spider's-web part of the dreamcatcher dotted around with turquoise stones and a quartz crystal bang in the middle, covering the bloody hole where the good dreams are supposed to get through in the first place! A wonderful way to piss on the culture you're cannibalising.

Because of the proliferation of such embarrassing tat, most Native Americans think dreamcatchers are as vulgar and disrespectful as those kitsch Jesus action figures and glow-in-the dark crucifixes are to Christians.

# Have a Powwow with American Indians

● ● ● ● ● ● ● ● ● ● ● ● ● ● ● ● ● ● ● ● ● ● ● ● ● ● ● ● ● ● ● ● ● ●

First things first, a powwow is not a peace conference between a big chief and some palefaces where everyone smokes a massive pipe and the chief says, 'We are all brothers under the skin, now hand over rifles and whisky!' It's a huge carnival, like an Eisteddfod or the Edinburgh Festival or cheese rolling in Gloucestershire, and has always been an excuse for different Native American tribes to get together and revel in their ethnicity, sing songs, dance dances and drink fire water. For a Westerner in search of some kind of spiritual enlightenment to turn up to one of these is a bit like a policeman or a vicar dancing at the Notting Hill Carnival. It's embarrassing, totally needless and wrong. Of course, the authentic tribespeople would be nice and friendly to you, but they'd probably prefer you to be doing what all the other whiteys were doing, such as slobbing around the mall all day, or shooting your classmates.

Let's just suppose the powwow is in some way like it was in TV westerns – a rare opportunity to sit down in an authentic setting, smoke some shit and chew the fat with a wise person who sees the world in a completely different way from you. Do you think Chief Silverheels is sitting there with um peace pipe, just dying to hear all the interesting things you have to say? All he wants to know is where he can get cheap gas for his pickup truck, better broadband speed from his wireless hub and why white folk drive around in Winnebagos when the word actually means 'people of the stinking water'. Although if he'd ever had to empty a chemical toilet from a caravan, he'd have his answer.

# Undergo a Rebirthing Experience

This is the kind of spiritual thrill that Cherie Blair used to force her husband to undergo on one of their uber-middle-class holidays, and was no doubt recommended to her by her 'guru' Carole Caplin. It's the kind of thing these people tack on to a holiday in the same way that you or I (or probably just I) would pay extra for a mackerel-fishing trip in Polperro.

There's a bizarre snobbery attached to mysticism and 'spirituality' these days which dismisses anything Western or Judaeo-Christian. Instead, for the seeker of enlightenment and inner wellbeing, only native tribesmen or a Third World shaman can cut it when it comes to reconnecting them with their true selves or the cosmos, or whatever. So whenever there's some Native American Indian, Mayan Indian or Indian Indian goodies on the spiritual smorgasbord, you can count the New Agers in.

Rebirthing (basically 'funny breathing') is described by devotees as the fastest way to get to your 'core issues'. Apparently, it helps you learn to relax and 'go deeper within yourself and thus farther into the body to experience the pleasure of you'. It's ironic how the inner workings of deep and meaningful 'therapies' like this are only ever described in sentences that are utterly meaningless.

I'll have a go at paraphrasing some of the orthodox thinking on this: We tend to make major life decisions based on our experiences of being born. By controlling our breathing we can experience 'rebirthing' and remember why we made those decisions and unblock the areas of our lives those decisions affect now.

In other words, if you keep breathing in such a weird way that you start to hyperventilate, you will eventually begin to hallucinate and then, whatever you think happened in the womb *did* happen, and whatever you've done in your life certainly wasn't your fault.

Now, I'm no expert on . . . well, anything at all, really, but I'm pretty sure that the attraction of the authentic religions of India, Mexico, Tibet, Nevada, or wherever, is rooted in something deeper than this. And what do you know? The whole Indian rebirthing palaver comes not from Mexico, Nepal or Ulan Batur; it comes from 1960s California.

A born-again Christian called Leonard Orr was wallowing in his bathtub in 1960, as was his wont, and suddenly remembered that he tried to strangle himself in the womb because he knew his mother didn't want him. Having released this 'psychic block' he could tap into his 'reservoir of divinity'. He then persuaded, with considerable success, it has to be said, many thousands more to lie in a bath with a snorkel and breathe themselves into better shape.

Mr Orr went on to become a respected figure in the world of New Age therapies, but you might say he slightly over-reached himself when he claimed that his way of breathing would actually make people physically immortal. To back this up he also claimed that in 1977 he had met and received endorsement from a physically immortal Yogi – Haidakhan Babaji:

'I asked Babaji: "Does rebirthing produce *mrityunjaya* (victory over death)?" Babaji replied: "Rebirthing produces *mahamrityunjaya* (supreme victory over death)." And that was all I needed – a confirmation of my theories from an actual immortal.'

Unfortunately, Babaji died in 1984. But you can see how Orr needed the benediction of a bona fide non-Western mystic – without it, rebirthing sounds like kooky nonsense from a crackpot Yank. But maybe that's actually a more believable provenance, because, oh dear, what's this? In 1950 a book was published anticipating Leonard Orr's theories by ten years: according to its author everybody's problems are caused by energy blocks or 'engrams' created in unborn children in the womb: 'Mama gets hysterical, baby gets an engram . . . each contains pain and unconsciousness'.

The book was called *Dianetics*, the author, L Ron Hubbard, the religion, Scientology. I won't say any more; I don't fancy being 'unblocked' by Tom Cruise and his band of zealots.

# Cut Your Child's Umbilical Cord

In Britain today there is a sinister fundamentalist movement trying to brainwash impressionable women. It's a sort of Childbirth Taliban. The tenets of this pseudo-religion include pain, humiliation, mind control and breathing exercises. Its devotees aim to return us to the Dark Ages and deny three centuries of advances in pain control, cleanliness, sanitation and respect for life. Actually, why stop at the Dark Ages? Why not take a tip from the Spartans and expose your newborn on a hillside? After all, he has to develop his own immune system, doesn't he?

All over Britain right now there are thousands of men trying to think up excuses to avoid going to natural childbirth classes with their wives. They've agreed to be present at the birth and they're hoping that, apart from a bit of hand holding and soaking up of verbal abuse, that's as far as it goes. But some fundamentalists want them to see the whole of the butcher's shop and have encouraged a range of gruesome practices to boot. 'Cutting the Umbilical Cord' goes hand in hand with the expectant parents swimming about in a paddling pool full of faecal matter and amniotic fluid. It's another of the ways we are encouraged to go back to nature, as if rummaging around in our own entrails is what we were always meant to do. We are not animals, we are much smarter and kinder, we don't eat with our feet, we wear underpants, we fly planes and we build cities.

Cutting the umbilical cord is favoured by the same people who refuse to give their children antibiotics - bollocks to you, Alexander Fleming and your stupid discovery; piss off, Pasteur, I'm going to let my child taste milk's natural TB goodness. These people seem to be under the impression that all the bad people are now working in hospitals and they're out to get us.

Yes, medical incompetence can kill, dirty wards can kill, injecting the wrong drug into the wrong body part can kill, but death in childbirth doesn't actually happen much these days. I was born at home because there was so much snow about that my parents couldn't get to hospital, but believe me, my dad would have carried my mum there if he'd been able. A midwife turned up on a bicycle. This was 1961 and I bet my mother wouldn't have said no to an epidural if they had reached the West Riding by then. But these days women are encouraged to shun epidurals in order to experience the 'positive pain' of childbirth, and cutting the cord is a conspiratorial move to get Dad involved in all this nonsense.

I have heard some men say it's a really moving experience, usually when their wives are within earshot, but it was all I could do to stay in the same room when my kids were delivered by caesarean (don't even breathe this word near the Childbirth Taliban). The puppet show as the kids were hoicked over the blue curtain was experience enough for me.

There was a national outcry recently when one father from Newcastle was prevented by hospital authorities from cutting his child's cord. He was quoted in the papers as saying, 'I think it is important from a bonding point of view. This is the only thing a father can do at the birth.' And what could possibly go wrong? Well, a few years' earlier, someone had actually chopped off a new-born baby's toe. That's why the hospital banned relatives from cutting the umbilical cord in the first place. Quite right. Why would you allow an untrained idiot anywhere near surgical instruments? I'm all for bans like that; feel free to ban me from operating theatres forever.

And what is all this 'bonding' business anyway? Most men understand bonding to be what you do with people at work who you don't like very much and it usually involves paint-balling. But no. Now it's all about what you have to do to forge a link with your newborn. But it's your chuffing baby for heaven's sake! If, in order to bond with your own flesh and blood, you feel you have to practise some weirdo, pagan, faery ring, tra-la-la-la witchcraft ceremony, then should you really be having children?

Some women now think having their men present actually *increases* the chance of 'intervention' and that this is down to the knight-in-shining-armour syndrome - men calling for the epidural/caesarean/pain relief in response to their instinctive urge to save their damsel in distress.

It's hard to believe, but a select group of nutters think that even removing the baby from inside the mother is the work of infidels. This is a genuine quote from an on-line fundamentalist:

'If I didn't think it was a baby's right to let go of their own cord, it would be my place to do it. But honestly, the thought of cutting through the connection with my baby makes me feel sick to my stomach . . . As far as I'm concerned a man has absolutely no place in separating me from my baby. Or separating my baby from its placenta-brother/sister. I would absolutely NEVER allow it, regardless of how much it meant to them.'

Brilliant - in a few years, if this kind of thinking takes hold, men will be able to return to their traditional role in childbirth, pacing up and down outside the hospital with a cigar, waiting for the happy event to be announced so they can bugger off down the pub to celebrate with their mates.

# Play on the Swings when You're a Grown-up

● ● ● ● ● ● ● ● ● ● ● ● ● ● ● ● ● ● ● ● ● ● ● ● ● ● ● ● ● ● ● ● ● ● ●

The desire to hang on to childhood is one of the main drivers of the 'things to do before you die' lists and 'Play on the Swings' is bound to be high on many of them, although why stop there? Why not 'make a daisy chain', 'paint your face like a tiger' and 'wet your bed at night-time'?

It's been a feature of the last twenty years, since the hippies became the Establishment, to try and blur the lines between grown-ups and kids. In the words of the Woodstock generation, we have to try and 'get back to the Garden'; the Eden we lost by wearing suits and working for a living. So on the one hand, you get knowing T-shirts for toddlers which say things like 'My mom's food sucks', 'More toys now or the puppy gets it' and 'My ISA just matured'. And on the other hand, you get adults trying to hide themselves in a den of perpetual childhood. Take a look at some of the up-market mail-order catalogues like 'Pedlars' or 'Boogaloo'. It's as if Freud decided to jack in the psychiatry game for something more profitable. Most of the stuff they are pitching to affluent 35-year-olds is from a long-lost toy cupboard:

metal wind-up robots, table-football games, Dansette record players, gardening tools that look like seaside toys and, the most alluring plaything for the man who has everything, except his youth – a drum kit (see 'Learn a Musical Instrument').

So what's wrong with playing on the swings and the slides and the other stuff in a playground when you're a grown-up? It's wrong because there are enough adults in playgrounds already, like drunks, drug addicts and paedos. Take a look at the graffiti on the climbing frame at your local playground – and thank God your kids can't read yet. Or look under the slide if you dare – the treasure trove ranges from empty cans of Tennent's to used syringes, used condoms and, occasionally, the scorched body of a tramp.

Suppose you are perfectly law-abiding and you go skipping off in your short trousers or pigtails to your nearest playground, what then? The slide is too narrow for your adult backside, your feet drag along underneath the swing and you're far too heavy to carry your own weight on the monkey bars. What kind of overgrown idiot do you look like?

But the main problem with adults larking about in playgrounds is that they are making a mockery of those who are there against their will. If you don't have children and you casually walk by a kid's playground you may not notice them, like Antony Gormley statues cemented around the perimeter, until one of them moves to pick a screaming toddler off the ground. It's mainly women in the week, men at weekends – a strange apartheid imposed on middle-class couples, based on the fact that, thanks to new technology, what the man does during the week cannot possibly be described as work. So he has to put in extra shifts on Saturday and Sunday, shivering and frowning and clutching his paper cup of expensive coffee and waiting for his uncoordinated toddler to fall off the climbing frame or bang their head on a swing seat.

Believe me, the last thing he wants to see is a couple of carefree, childless 29-year-olds goofing around on the mini-roundabout, cackling and pulling funny faces before they wander off to while away the afternoon in a pub, the bastards.

# Go Dancing in the Rain

Like 'Skinny-Dipping' (see p. 175) and 'Drinking Champagne out of a Slipper' (see p. 70), dancing in the rain is what you do if you want to say to the world: 'Do you know what? I just don't care what people think about me – I'm completely mad.'

If you put 'dancing in the rain' into YouTube, you'll find quite a lot of outdoor shimmying and shaking in poor weather; it's invariably performed by girls in their late teens or early twenties and I think it's part of an elaborate mind-game/courtship ritual. A man might join in with a spot of rain dancing if he thought he might cop off with the girl who suggested it, and that's exactly what the rain-dance ladies are after – a demonstration of irrational behaviour. I think young women have been heavily influenced by romantic comedies they've watched on DVD with a bottle of wine and some chocolates. In the relevant scene, The Girl can often be found shaking her head fondly at the crazy antics of The Boy, as he demonstrates how 'mad' he is about her, either by sitting in a bath full of water or running along the roofs of cars in a traffic jam to get to her or, as in the film *Truly, Madly, Deeply*, hopping on one leg for twenty minutes while he chats her up. In every case, the girl smiles at him and the audience thinks, 'Hey! He's just crazy enough to make her happy.' But she's not really after a crazy bloke – that could end up in all sorts of horrible ways – what she really wants is a man who can demonstrate the potential for irrational behaviour, because this will help in the later stages of a relationship when she is planning to do something unnecessary and inconvenient, like repainting the living room a slightly creamier shade of beige. If the man objects on the grounds that no sane person could possibly tell the difference between one colour and the other, she can reply with, 'Well, you don't always do the normal thing, what about when you went dancing in the rain with me?' And so the trap is sprung. Dancing in the rain is to be avoided at all costs. I can't think of any decent excuse for a man to dance in the rain, unless maybe you are Tim Robbins in *The Shawshank Redemption* and you've just dug yourself out of prison with a spoon, or you are Gene Kelly and you are in a film whose title song goes 'I'm dancing and singin' in the rain'.

# Go Skinny-dipping

One of the best lines in the film *Butch Cassidy and the Sundance Kid* is at the end when they are holed up in the Bolivian village and Butch tells Sundance they should go to Australia, where he could learn to swim; Sundance replies, 'No swimming! It's not important!' Even at the point of death Sundance knows the truth: that immersing your body in deep water is stupid, dangerous and scary. Swimming is way too unpleasant to start with, without bringing nudity into it.

Apart from the fact that it involves swimming, there are other problems with skinny-dipping. Number one, there's the rude-health freakery of it: it's a telltale sign of a military upbringing or a public school education. 'Yes! A naked swim in freezing cold water – the perfect way to round off cadet manoeuvres before chapel!'

Not long ago a Muslim boy was actually expelled from his private school for refusing to go swimming in the nude – it was deemed to be so integral to the education of young boys that it took precedence over religious observance, and it's just the kind of thing they forced Prince Charles to do when he was imprisoned at Stalag Gordonstounluft, which probably explains a lot.

Seasoned skinny-dippers will bang on about how unnatural it is to cover up the body and that it's only a matter of time before we shed all swimwear, pointing to how tiny the bikinis and Speedos are now compared to the encumbrances of Victorian bathing costumes. Really, I wish they'd get over it; naturists lost the clothing battle several thousand years ago. The notion of 'covering your modesty' is frequently ridiculed but the shrivelled privates of a naked swimmer are far more ridiculous.

But these people are a different strain of nude swimmer to the most annoying and dangerous kind – the spontaneous skinny-dipper. The kind of person who likes to 'tear up the rule book' and defy convention. They are the sort who will moon without warning or get their tits out after a couple of Bacardi

Breezers. And the women are just as bad. You see them in 'steamy' TV dramas where the snogging couple are so taken up with the heat of the moment that they knock things off the shelves and the table – it's usually a kitchen table – so the ketchup goes over and the milk bottle smashes, etc. Now who would let that kind of thing happen and not get distracted? Certainly no woman I know.

The spontaneous skinny-dipper will only have to smell the sea or spot a narrow boat gliding down a canal before the kit starts peeling off; but despite their love of living in the moment, their lack of foresight will eventually catch up with them and they'll regret it afterwards. First of all, they won't have a towel – it's spontaneous, you see? So they'll have to put their clothes back on while they're still wet; that's never pleasant – everything clings and gathers and rouches and feels really uncomfortable. It's when they're struggling with the clothes that they are likely to discover they have bit of vegetation or plastic bag or condom or scum and froth stuck to a leg, and if they have spontaneously skinny-dipped with some other people they may well discover – too late – that they have got their pants mixed up.

All these things I witnessed the one time I was almost lured into an evening of skinny-dipping by a girl at school – it wasn't Jacqueline Stebbings this time, it was Louise Mullroy, who had a very persuasive way about her. On one unchaperoned sixth-form trip to Blackpool, she had me and three other youths twitching in her spider's web. After several drinks on the seafront she declared she was going to swim naked and was anyone else going to join her? Three did, one didn't. My innate sense of what was cool and what wasn't persuaded me not to. That and the fact that I couldn't then – nor can I now – swim a stroke. If I'd followed Louise Mullroy in her foamy frolicking I would quite probably have been toppled over by a tiny wave and either panicked, flapped and snorted like a small child, or very quickly drowned. In any event, I would have lost face in front of her and there was no way that was going to happen. No – I was saving my massive Louise Mullroy embarrassment for the sixth-form disco two weeks later. But on the beach at Blackpool I took the wise counsel of the Sundance Kid and told myself – 'Naked swimming! It's not important.'

# **Build a Bonfire on a Beach**

● ● ● ● ● ● ● ● ● ● ● ● ● ● ● ● ● ● ● ● ● ● ● ● ● ● ● ● ● ● ● ●

Apart from the carbon emissions and certain specific bylaws forbidding fires on beaches, I suppose I don't have much against this one except that it is what Catholics call 'an occasion of sin', meaning it might well lead to other bad stuff – usually, in this case, hippy behaviour. People are prone to stare into fires, especially on beaches, and start saying stupid things and telling stories about elves.

Most beach-based fireside behaviour is predictable. It won't matter how big the fire is, the flames could be leaping twenty feet in the air and peeling the skin off your face, but some girl will be too cold and ask to borrow your jumper. Two of your group will get off with each other, seduced by the flickering light, and the clingy lovers will gather up some sand and pebbles and seashells in a seaside bucket and keep it with them as a reminder of their coastal tryst forever and ever, or at least until they split up a week later. No one will have brought any food. Eventually someone will put on a hat like this:

Someone will then get a guitar out – it used to be 'Kumbaya' that everyone dreaded (it's still quite lethal) but now it's 'Losing My Religion' or 'Angie' by the Rolling Stones or 'Wonderwall' or 'No Woman No Cry' or something by Simon and Garfunkel – 'The Boxer', probably. No one ever gets a guitar out next to a bonfire on the beach and sings anything by the Undertones or Blondie or Madness.

Obviously none of this applies in Australia, where it's never cold and outdoor fire lighting is on the national curriculum. And, of course, the idea that an Australian would be within a mile of an outdoor fire without food or drink is preposterous. And if that wasn't enough, they're so offensively sociable. It's like being at a party in a house full of rugby players and female estate agents, where you would normally avoid any social intercourse by pretending to examine the host's CD collection or lurk around the food table. Except the trouble with Australian outdoor fire parties (I find the word 'barbie' offensive) is that there is no kitchen to hide in – all the food is alight or over hot coals and wrapped in tin foil.

No matter where the beach fire, even after most of the revellers have gone and left their carbonised crap half-buried in the sand for someone's horse to tread on, there will still be a couple of people left determined to fulfil their ambition to . . .

# Stay up All Night on a Beach until Sunrise

Some people are slightly obsessed with staying up until the sun rises. I don't think it necessarily has to take place on a beach, although as you've seen, lots of 'things to do before you die' involve beaches. Adding the beach bit always seems to give the enterprise extra cachet, a bit like Olympic diving when somebody does a dive 'with pike'. I don't know what that means but it always impresses the judges.

Anyway, watching the sun come up is something you will have experienced if you've ever had bad toothache or a baby – pretty much the same thing for a lot of people – but that feeling of despair, after a sleepless night, at the dawn of a new day, is not shared by 'livers of life to the full'.

For these people, if you stay awake all night *de facto* you've had a brilliant time. You will have had so many interesting things to say to each other, so much in common, the hours will have flown by and before you know it – hey, let's go and have breakfast! But if you're really honest, most of you will have been desperate to go home for ages and are either too knackered to stand up, or can't bear the possibility of missing something amaaazing or that whoever's left will talk about you. I have to confess that, whenever possible, at these late-night chat-ins I have always pretended to be in a catatonic-style deep sleep to avoid having to express my true feelings and fall out with everyone. I would recommend this as a ploy, but very few people have believed I could possibly fall asleep when they were all being so interesting. So, over the years, my fake slumber has provoked severe kickings, hot wax, felt-pen whiskers drawn on my face and the word 'wanker' written on my forehead. On the plus side, it has got me out of at least two failing relationships.

But even supposing you had such a fantastic night and made friendships that will last forever, the next two days will be completely written off, as your brain and body try to recover. You will look like shit and be useless in meetings and annoying to your work colleagues. We've all wanted to punch someone whose only excuse for dullness and incompetence is 'Yeah, it was wicked, I didn't get to bed till six-thirty'.

Then on the journey home, which you've longed for since you staggered into the office, you'll fall asleep on the train and travel way past your stop, drooling and nodding and occasionally jolting awake going 'bloooaaaargh!' and hoping nobody noticed. As you walk into your kitchen, which hasn't been tidied for days because you've been up all night at someone else's house, or beach, you'll say to yourself 'If only I'd gone to bed at midnight I'd have had eight hours' sleep'. And then I hope you'll ask yourself the question which I've been trying to drum into you for 182 pages: 'Was it *really* worth it?'

# Have a Weekend of Pampering at a Health Spa

Is there a more annoying word in the English language than 'pampering'? Only 'detox' and 'Brangelina' come close. Maybe I find it annoying because it's what people call a 'girlie' thing: a weekend of pampering is always referred to in the likes of *Heat* and *Grazia* as a *must* for 'the girls'. I can just hear Denise Welch on *Loose Women* saying, 'We all need a bit of pampering, don't we, girls?'

'Pampering' used to be quite clearly a bad thing – along with indulging, mollycoddling, spoiling and other ways of turning children into brats. But now, pampering and self-indulgence have become highly desirable and, appropriately, cost a fortune.

As far as I can tell from health spa brochures and websites, pampering involves dressing up in stupidly oversized towelling dressing gowns, spreading fruit on your face and having someone punch you in the back for 250 quid a day. Women I know who are usually pretty canny about how they spend money seem to take all leave of their senses when it comes to health spas. But then the practitioners of pampering know exactly which fiendishly seductive words work like catnip on the female psyche.

Try these, ladies:

- Luxurious mineralising muds
- Egyptian cleansing ritual
- Balinese hot stone massage
- Energising wrap
- Deep tissue therapy
- Hydration-enhancing moisture surge
- Full Rasul–Moroccan experience (?)
- Retinol with active liposomes

Actually, that last bit was nicked from the wordsmiths at Laboratoire Garnier, but you get the picture. I could probably charge some women 200 quid just for reading that lot out loud. And what concerns me is the fine line between suggesting something sensual, even a little bit naughty, and proposing something downright pornographic.

Take massages:

- Turkish Massage – just the right side of the line
- Swedish Massage – nudge nudge
- Thai Massage – phnaar!
- French Massage – dodgy shop window
- Nigerian Massage – no way
- Belgian Massage – a euphemism for something pretty disgusting.

Is this what women really want? Do they really have such stressful lives that some rudimentary physiotherapy and a bit of witch-doctoring constitutes the height of luxury?

Frankly, ladies, I'm disappointed. Yes, men may be useless tosspots in many ways, but no man I know would fall for the pampering con trick because, leaving aside the senseless waste of money, there's just nothing in it for them. You do come across the odd attempt at pampering-for-him services, but all these really amount to is a shave with a hot towel. Most men know that you don't actually need to spend a fortune to achieve total relaxation and inner peace – all you need is an armchair, some cans and a television.

# Eat at the Best Restaurant in the World

The holder of this title may change depending on when you come across this book (is this a nice Oxfam? – be polite to the old lady) but in the middle of the first decade of the 21st century it is consistently a place called El Bulli in Spain. So it's a really posh, expensive restaurant that you probably have to dress up for and it's in another country – the signs are not promising, are they?

El Bulli is only open for six months of the year and there's only a one in a hundred chance of getting a table, so you can see why a certain type of person would be suckered into going there. They would also fall for *Restaurant* magazine's reason for awarding the prize: 'The food at El Bulli demands psychological reflection. In other words, you don't come to El Bulli for a feed, you come for an experience.'

I'm always suspicious of the word 'experience' being included in anything other than a job advert. When it's applied to anything else my bullshit detector kicks into overdrive – e.g. the West Wittering Dinosaurs Experience, the London Dungeon

Experience, the Durham Mining Museum Pit Shaft Experience and – believe it or not, in Orlando – the Holy Land Experience, so that you can imagine what it was like in Israel in Biblical times. Or you could just go to Israel.

However sensational the food at El Bulli may be, the level of bullshit surrounding it is world class. It's website declares that 'the barriers between the sweet and savoury world are being broken down'. I wonder if they are talking about fruit with meat? If so, count me out – ham and pineapple? duck and orange? pork and apple? – eurgh! I really don't fancy spending 250 euros per head on this sort of stuff if there's a chance I'm not going to like it. Actually, it turns out that some of the flavour combinations at El Bulli are even more outrageous than that:

*Baby broad beans with ham, prawns and lamb's brain garnish*

My first concern would be, 'Will I be able to pick the chewy bits out?' or 'Will they let me have that without the lamb's brain?'

Poncy restaurants always do this to you – you read the description of the dish from the menu and say to yourself, 'Salmon? Yes, I like that. A herb crust? And that. Ooh, garlic mashed potato, that sounds nice . . . oh – "garnished with anchovy hats" – they've gone and spoiled it.' But this kind of thing is El Bulli's raison d'être. Look at this:

*Raspberry kebab with balsamic caramel cloud*

I don't know whether to laugh or explode with rage. There was a Mike Leigh film many years ago in which Timothy Spall played a restaurant owner in the 1980s who was experimenting with nouvelle cuisine. He came up with such unlikely combinations as 'Saveloys with Lychees' and 'Liver in Lager'. In the film he is a deluded fool, but at El Bulli they are 'breaking down the product–garnish–sauce hierarchy'. There's more:

*Frozen yogurt and extra virgin olive oil lolly*
*Sardines with blackcurrant and eucalyptus*
*Sweetcorn nitro foam with black truffle jus jelly and duck foie gras air*

The rave reviews of this restaurant proclaim the explosions of taste and varieties of sensations in the mouth to be like nothing the reviewers have ever experienced before, but the way they describe it sounds to me like the effect of Space Dust on a child's mouth. Here's my favourite:

*Goose Barnacles with Albarino Sabayon*

I have absolutely no idea what it means but I think Chelsea should sign them straight away.

A *Guardian* journalist, sent to review the restaurant, wrote that anyone who was shocked or surprised by the El Bulli experience was 'either a fool or an unsophisticate'. What an inelegant way to express snobbery.

I like posh food; I like the occasional fancy restaurant, but I am also entitled not to eat what I don't like the sound of. A A Gill – a sadly underrated writer – said each one of us is probably going to have only a hundred meals out in a lifetime (unless you're a journalist) and we ought to make each occasion somewhere special; for their part the restaurant is obliged to make us feel special and the whole event worth the money. Dead right – so if a restaurant is taking my money it has no right to any judgement on the sophistication of my palate and if I want more salt they should bloody well fetch it. Maybe they do at El Bulli. But even if I had a fabulous evening and had the best meal of my life there, I think there is a limit to what can legitimately be spent on recreational food – 200 quid per person for dinner might be worth it to the individual who eats it, if it is truly spectacular, but like the lady on the TV property show who spent £1,000 on a tap, it's an affront to the rest of the world.

# Run A Marathon

We all know a lot of money is raised for charity by sponsored marathon runners, but we also know that's not the only reason they do it. They do it because they want you to say to them, 'Oh wow, you've run a marathon, that's amazing! How long did it take you? I could never do that!'

Running 26 miles and 385 yards somehow elevates them

above someone like me who hasn't run anywhere for twenty years or who gets a bit puffed out walking upstairs. It's almost universally regarded as a true measure of what man can achieve if he really tries; if you can run a marathon you have proved your worth to the human race, you've pushed the boundaries of physical endurance, discovered a lot about yourself, been on a learning curve, ad nauseum, add nausea. In reality, though, it's just another thing to tick off from your list of achievements on mylife'sbetterthanyours.com.

The marathon runner's smugness begins way before they've crossed the finish line and been enveloped in tinfoil by Jimmy Saville. The training is actually much more useful as a bragging tool than running the race – that's over in one day; training can last years. The other great thing about marathon training is the Implied Superior Fitness Even In Failure. 'Had a bad run this morning. Hit the wall at ten-K.' You're meant to react by admitting you could never run ten-K if your life depended on it and of course ask what they mean by 'the wall'.

Please don't ever give them the satisfaction; please, not the bloody wall, the wall of pain, the chuffing pain barrier! Some religions get a lot of stick for glorifying pain and making a virtue out of suffering, but I'd point the finger much more usefully at sport. How many times do we hear sports journalists or athletes bang on about 'playing through the pain', 'feeling the burn' or 'hitting the wall'? I can distinctly remember David Coleman at some big event (or maybe it was just the Commonwealth Games) describing a British athlete's heroic failure:'Here comes David Jenkins and he hits the bend in a sea of lactic acid!' And I could just imagine the experienced runners nodding approvingly: 'Mmm, that lactic acid; it really knacks.'

Sport is one long celebration of injury – shin splints, groin strains, pulled hamstrings, tennis elbow and, of course, jogger's nipple; just one of the many delights on offer to the long-distance runner: nipples rubbed to buggery by four hours' friction on a nylon vest. Or you might prefer to lose a couple of toenails, which is pretty common for new runners, but not as common as the diarrhoea which often follows or even accompanies the jarring of the abdomen for 26 miles. Not the kind of trots many first-time marathon runners bargained for, I'm sure. And all in full view of cheering crowds. Why are they there, anyway? What are they looking at? Well, according to the BBC's London Marathon website: 'It makes gripping viewing for the armchair observer, as the wobbly-legged brigade hobble over the finish line, their faces contorted in pain.'

Sounds brilliant, doesn't it? I honestly can't see the appeal in thousands of pallid ectomorphs loping around like something out of *The Corpse Bride*, spilling liquid out of paper cups, with their bony elbows and stinky feet, shitting themselves as they run. And don't get me started on the people dressed hilariously as gorillas and polar bears, and the Breakfast TV reporters, chosen by their producers to run because they're 'characters' and because it's all just 'a bit of fun'. The word 'fun' crops up a lot in long-distance running – 'It's a great day out, it's a Fun Run'. I'd say Fun Run is as much a contradiction in terms as 'end-of-the-pier humour', 'military intelligence' or 'Express Newspapers'.

So why even think of long-distance running? Who dreamed it up?

Well, the founders of the modern Olympic movement were actually inspired by an old Robert Browning poem to include a 26-mile running race in the first Olympics in 1896. But there is literally and historically no point to the marathon. It's a made-up event; it never featured in the Olympics in Ancient Greece. There is no historical testimony to back up the story that somebody, call him Pheidippides or Philippides or Papadopoulos, ever actually ran 26 miles anywhere in Ancient Greece; nor is there any agreement where this mythical person started from or finished. Whoever it was, or wasn't, they were supposed to have run from the Battle of Marathon to Athens 26 miles away, to tell them of the great victory over the Persians, and then dropped dead. But what would have been the point of that? You don't need a desperate dash to tell someone some good news; surely it would've waited? You wouldn't want all the stay-at-homes and armchair patriots whooping it up and drinking all the ouzo before your actual front-line troops have made it home. If it had been a terrible defeat you could understand. 'Go on, Pheidippidos, or whatever your name is, tell the Athenians we've been given a proper kicking, the Persians are on their way so everyone had better scarper.' But even then you'd send a horse if you were really in a hurry, wouldn't you? People who have heard of him always refer to Herodotus, the first historian (or tabloid journalist, depending on your point of view), describing the original Marathon in 490 BC, but actually, he doesn't. He says someone called Pheidippides ran the 150 miles from Athens to Sparta in two days (yeah, right) to ask them to come to the Athenians' aid against the Persians. But the Spartans wouldn't go because there wasn't a full moon, so that tells you what they thought about long-distance running.

Even though it's a totally made-up sporting event with no purpose and is frankly a bit ridiculous, we are supposed to contemplate the marathon and ask ourselves, 'Could I do it? Dare I discover the truth about myself?'

If it was in any way worthwhile or beneficial to mankind, I'd ask, 'Could I do it?' If I was thinking about fighting for my country, or helping someone in the street who's being attacked, I'd ask, 'Could I do it?' But I don't think it's a measure of anyone's worth to buy some expensive trainers and hobble around London like a pensioner trying to catch a bus. For me, the only good thing to come out of marathon running is the film *Marathon Man*. It's really quite good. I'd recommend it, but obviously, feel free not to bother, it's only quite good.

# Build Your Own House

If anything flies directly in the face of the *Can't Be Arsed* ethos, it's this. Building your own house has to be the most time-consuming, expensive, stressful undertaking ever. When I was younger and more stupid I did up two houses, one after the other; renovated them from top to bottom. Fortunately, I have a handy wife and an even handier father-in-law. We've ended up with a nice house, probably worth more than we paid for it, although by the time I've reached the end of this sentence it will have dropped another couple of grand. Was it worth it? No, not really; in total it took about three years of my life, I'll never get that time back, and if I see one more Rawlplug I'll have to kill someone.

But building a house from *scratch* is much more of a nightmare proposition and you only have yourself to blame if it goes wrong. You can't blame Victorian builders, careless previous owners, incompetent surveyors or dodgy estate agents. If the four walls don't join up to the roof, if the soil pipe discharges into the washing machine, it's all your fault. And the stress would be compounded by Kevin McCloud from *Grand Designs* frowning at the camera in a hard hat, saying, 'It's a beautiful timber-frame construction but I'm wondering if Peter and Sarah can maintain the integrity of the space . . .'

Programmes like *Grand Designs*, though they are the ultimate in middle-class television, have done those very same viewers a great disservice by making them (OK, us) feel that building our dream house is easily within our grasp. Right now there are probably dozens of couples emailing Kevin McCloud and asking him to film their eco-friendly modernist-gothic windmill. I'm always amazed that people on the show manage to finish their immaculate and spectacular self-build houses for about a third of what it cost to buy mine, but the fact remains that whether you are renovating or building a new house you are often gambling for a couple of years with at least half a million pounds. Time multiplied by Money = Pain in the Arse.

# Learn a Language

If you must learn a language, there is no point sitting in a classroom or listening to CDs in the car or watching a DVD at home; the only way to learn a language properly is to go and live in a country and immerse yourself in its people and culture for at least a year. Now that's not going to happen, is it?

It's a waste of time learning a European language anyway, because in a few years even the French will have learned sufficient English for a total dunderhead to communicate with them. Outside of Europe . . . well, I think we've established that it's way too much trouble to venture that far, so we can forget about learning Chinese or anything like that. It would actually do the Chinese good to learn more English as they increase their contact with the West – words and phrases like 'human rights abuse', 'mass executions' and 'despicable' could be particularly useful to them. It would be a great leap forward for the whole world if we could develop an international language that *everyone* could speak. Not Esperanto, obviously – that was useless and even more complicated than the languages it was intended to replace. I'm suggesting Pictionary Drawing. Everyone always has to carry with them a pen and a notepad, and if you want to ask a foreigner for something, you just draw a picture of it and point to it repeatedly until he understands. It's simple, effective, and, above all, great fun. The only problem I haven't solved is what to do if the egg timer runs out and he hasn't got the answer?

# Learn A Musical Instrument

· · · · · · · · · · · · · · · · · · · · · · · · · · · · · · · · · · · ·

At last, something actually worth doing. Learning a musical instrument is one of the few self-indulgent things you can do that is really worthwhile. If you're good at it, you might even entertain other people, but even if you're a ham-fisted amateur playing on your own and it's someone else's music, you are at least communing with another human being in some way. Using the *Can't Be Arsed* formula of Time multiplied by Money divided by Sense of Anticlimax, learning an instrument is about the only thing in this book to come out with a decent score, so in theory it looks as if I will have to allow this one.

But which instrument? The piano is probably top of the list – everyone wishes they could play the piano well, but unless you have application, dedication and, most importantly, time, you haven't got a hope. William Hague took up the piano in his mid-forties and apparently he's really quite good now, but he hasn't got any kids, so when he gets home after a hard day's Deputy-Leader-of-the-Opposition-ing, he can get to work on his five-finger exercises.

Most instruments – cello, oboe, clarinet, trumpet, saxophone, trombone, harp, harpsichord, sackbut, crumhorn, zither, bazouki – are pretty much beyond the scope of grown-ups, who can't be forced by fear of exams or the high expectation of parents to practise for the requisite number of hours per day. You really need to crack this by about fourteen and if you haven't you may as well give up.

Which leaves the two instruments which, when picked up in later life, especially by an older man, betray a desperate attempt to hang on to one's youth – the guitar and the drums.

Men who 'have everything' get drums as presents – they look great but sound terrible. If you are one of these types, take heed. After a week you won't know what to do with them; your neighbours will hate you unless you cover them with a sheet, in which case you might as well play the arm of the sofa with some knitting needles. You will then realise that you can't do much other than play along to records and half the time you drown out the accompanying track (you could get a set of synth drums, but imagine yourself thumping some oversized plastic 50p pieces with headphones on, pretending you're Keith Moon – ridiculous). So you join a band of other sad dads, rehearsing in stinky studios under railway arches or perhaps even gigging in even dingier pubs to an unappreciative audience. Whatever you do you'll never escape the tyranny of the drums, which sit there, after you've given your all physically, demanding to be dismantled and put in a car (no matter how you try to configure it, you will have to fold the seat down) and driven home, while the guitarists put their axes in cases and get smashed before jumping in a cab.

Ah yes, guitars! Again, they look fantastic, don't they? Is there a more attractive thing to see hanging up in a shop window than an electric guitar (other than a sign saying 'Free beer and pies')? Of course, you'll have to buy an amp and a tutorial booklet; probably *Play in a Day* by Bert Weedon – everyone learned from that: Hank Marvin, Jimmy Page, Slash (well, maybe not Slash). The first couple of pages are easy: you play a few open strings and suddenly you're doing the Big Ben chimes; next there's a one-finger chord shape – G7 yeah, brilliant! You're getting quite excited now, then you turn the next page and you're faced with a blizzard of dots and squiggles more complex and difficult to understand than Linear B and the Rosetta Stone. So you give up trying to play properly and eventually figure out 'Smoke on the Water', the Status Quo twelve-bar thing, a fumbled bit of Led Zeppelin and maybe, after about two years, a Hendrix riff. You then leave the guitar leaning up against a corner in your living room for guests to admire when they come round. They'll say, 'Oh, do you play the guitar?' and you'll go, 'Nah . . .'

So although in principle learning an instrument is worth the effort, the practicalities are such that the Sense of Anticlimax factor grows exponentially with the expectation of your own performance level. For lazy, poorly motivated people, the only hope is that Rolf Harris may be persuaded to re-launch the Stylophone.

# Learn Circus Skills

• • • • • • • • • • • • • • • • • • • • • • • • • • • • • • • • • •

Running away from home to join a circus was a well-trodden path to asserting your independence in the kind of books I read when I was a kid. It all seemed so exciting – you'd mix with a troupe of crazy, eccentric, talented characters and some would hide dark secrets of crime and skulduggery. Best of all they'd teach you how to tightrope-walk, catch cannonballs, tame lions and jump through a hoop while on horseback. Sadly, circuses aren't like that any more – they are animal-friendly (i.e. no animals) and have a lot of juggling, leotards and mime. These are the circus skills of today – flag-throwing, streamer-twirling, juggling, fire-eating, stilt-walking, face-painting and living statues. Now be honest, as you read that list your heart sank, didn't it? Virtually any day out can be ruined by face-painting, juggling or living statues. Particularly Craft Fairs and Car Boot Sales. These are pretty dismal events to start with, but the sight of little kids being turned into tigers or a silver man standing still for three hours will really put the tin hat on it. Can you imagine anyone running away to a circus and shouting defiantly at their parents, 'I'm off to become a living statue!'

The heavy-duty circus stuff – the trapeze artistry and the tightrope walking and the human-pyramid building have now left behind the canvas tents and the greasepaint and, along with paintballing, go-karting and white-water rafting, are all used in team bonding sessions for middle management – 'D'you see, guys? You can't build the pyramid without everyone working together at the bottom!'

So, if you want to learn the old-fashioned, traditional skills you will have to be prepared to sit alongside Alex, Dave, Tim, Gary and Steve from Marketing.

Or there's one other way – you can join the Scouts. Believe it or not there is a scouting badge which covers high-wire walking, trapeze, tumbling, acrobatics and clowning.

So, circus skills – as favoured by corporate awayday tossers, face-painting crusties in a field or a paramilitary organisation for children. Hardly aspirational, is it?

# Perform Stand-up Comedy

●●●●●●●●●●●●●●●●●●●●●●●●●●●●●●●●●●●●●

I can just hear the howls of rage from all those people who have spent the last fifteen years working up material, honing an act and grubbing around the stand-up circuit for fifty quid a gig. It's bad enough when some ponces from Cambridge walk straight into their own Radio 4 show, having never been near the upstairs room of a grotty pub in Camberwell, but the idea of even half a dozen people browsing their Internet 'to do list' and thinking: 'Yeah, stand-up comedy – I'll do that one this week', would make your average three-gigs-a-night comedian explode.

This comedian probably started thinking about stand-up as a young lad (it's a 90 per cent male occupation). He will have been inspired by his TV comedy heroes and will probably have a close group of friends who think he's quite funny, or can remember a lot of jokes, at least. A bit like a young Morrissey, he'll spend his teenage years alone in his bedroom, while other kids are doing their homework, getting into university, practising magic tricks or having sex with someone. He'll be thinking about routines, set-ups, punch lines and put-downs and imagining how that first gig will go. It might take him five years to pluck up the courage to perform; he'll get an open spot and be humiliated and abused by some drunks. How he reacts to that experience will decide his fate. A lot of people like him will have plenty of quick wit, a facility with language and varying combinations of anger, bile and spite, but deep down they know they are not sufficiently unhinged to carry on, so they become gag writers. Some give up comedy completely, but a hard core persevere. A tiny fraction make decent money and even a TV career out of it, but the rest are foot soldiers in the war against an unappreciative audience; what one uncompromising comedian used to call 'the granite-faced spastics'.

(Of course, the Cambridge ponce won't have to do any of that. Cambridge has a specially designed syllabus for guaranteeing employment in radio and television, which includes a module on stand-up. If he completes the required number of performances in the 'Snooters' or whatever they call it, he gets an Equity Card, his own radio show and a development deal with Pixar, which will help pay the mortgage while he tops the bill at Jongleurs.)

The first successful modern stand-up was Alexei Sayle, whose attitude could be summed up as: 'Anyone can make an audience laugh if the audience likes them. The real test is if you can make them hate you and still make them laugh.'

This goes to illustrate a couple of things about stand-ups. One: inside their heads they are not quite normal. Two: it's fair to say they have an unusual relationship with their audience.

Anyone who thinks they can do stand-up even once should remember that no one is more hated than the person who gets up onstage and isn't funny. I had to get up at a 'do' once, just to introduce a comedian, and the audience's mood was so obvious they might as well have held up placards. 'How dare you think you're funny. How dare you stand up in front of me and think you can make me laugh, and how dare you embarrass me by not doing so. Why don't you fuck off and die?'

If you're a new act on the bill, the audience would like to kill you; the only way for you to survive is to kill them. Even established comics have to deal with it, that's why they talk about 'dying' and 'killing'. Some comedy agents don't just go looking for funny people, they go looking for killers.

If you insist on insulting hundreds of impoverished but dedicated, driven performers by 'having a go at stand-up' for a night, at least do a bit of research. First of all, choose the right name. You'll find most comedians are called Mark or Lee or

Alan. I haven't just picked those names because there are famous stand-ups called Mark, Lee, and Alan – just go to Chortle, the comedy website, and look down the list at the dozens of Marks, Lees, and Alans. Anyway, you might want to choose a different name if you want to stand out but please don't make it a jokey one; I was once given a genuine business card by a comedian called Tommy Laff.

Most successful comics will tell you that it takes about two years to learn how to walk on stage as if you haven't just shat yourself, so what hope have you got for one night only? I know nothing of stagecraft or theatres or acting or any of the performing arts but there are some pretty obvious mistakes to avoid.

Don't do observations. Don't say, 'Has anyone ever noticed …?' 'Has anyone ever noticed that it's not funny just because it's true?'

Don't say, while strolling around the stage, pretending to make it up as you go along, 'What else has been in the papers this week?' That's normally a signal that you are going to throw out some old stuff about what was in the papers three weeks ago.

Don't say, 'What's that all about?' when everyone knows what it's all about; as in "Star Wars – what's that all about?"

Don't do routines about air travel or why cats are cooler than dogs. Don't say, 'Weren't Aztec Bars brilliant?' or 'Do you remember *The Tomorrow People*?' Don't curry favour with orthodox lefties. Don't say Americans are stupid war criminals just because you know everyone will cheer and applaud. The truth is the Americans are actually very clever and invented everything in the entire bloody world and they don't behead people on video. Nobody believes in all that *Socialist Worker* guff any more, they just say they do because they think everyone else does. How else did Boris Johnson become Mayor of London?

Don't use the guise of a character to say all sorts of politically incorrect stuff about the disabled and the mentally ill – there's enough of that on TV. If you're going to be controversial and do offensive material, have the courage of your convictions; don't hide behind irony. Bernard Manning was deeply unpleasant but at least pretended to be nothing else.

Don't encourage anyone to whoop. Whooping is not what we do here and if we can stamp it out at grass-roots comedy-club level this country may have a chance of surviving.

I think what I'm trying to say is, don't do stand-up at all. There are plenty of comedians out there already and there can't be that much new material. It was once said that there are, in fact, only five basic jokes, to which Ken Dodd replied, 'If that's true, how come my act lasts three hours?' I'm sure three hours of Ken Dodd would tempt me to self-immolate, but I'd rather watch Ken's act through the smoke of my own burning flesh than the half-cocked musings of a to-do-list box-ticker who's just 'having a go'.

# Write a Book

● ● ● ● ● ● ● ● ● ● ● ● ● ● ● ● ● ● ● ● ● ● ● ● ● ● ● ● ● ● ● ●

I love books. I love bookshops. Large collections of books are particularly good to look at. Who wouldn't want their own library, a whole room in the house with sliding ladders and galleried stacks of titles reaching right up to the ceiling? Of course, there is no way you could read them all in your lifetime. Walk into any bookshop; take a look, just at the fiction section, and you are looking into the future, way beyond your own death.

So don't try adding to the bloody sum total then!

Never mind books, I don't have enough life left to listen to all the records and CDs I already own and that's not a huge number. It's the same with TV – there's already too much I haven't seen and no point in making any more. Look at how many DVDs of brilliant TV shows and amazing films are now available for next to nothing. How do you know where to start (since all prescriptive lists telling you what to watch or listen to before you die are going to be abolished by me)?

In one of the best TV series ever made, Anthony Soprano Junior tries to commit suicide and is asked by his analyst if he's ever thought of writing about his experience. He gives the perfect reply: 'Why would I do that?'

There is a view among therapists that writing down your own story or feelings or whatever, whether it's published or not, will be a positive experience for you, therapeutic even.

*The No Diet Diet* (given away free with the *Independent* newspaper early in 2008 when they'd run out of wall charts) even claimed it would help you lose weight!

'Write something for fifteen minutes . . . a story perhaps, or a poem or maybe the start of your own life story . . . over time it helps clarify the way you want to live. By writing for fifteen minutes you've taken another step towards freeing your soul and losing weight.'

I've met a few writers. Guess what? Many of them are fat. And in fifteen minutes, most of them will have made three cups of tea, moved some papers around, checked out their rivals' sales on Amazon, walked about a bit, eaten half a packet of biscuits and sighed deeply six times. And I'm not convinced that writing ever conferred a tremendous sense of wellbeing on the likes of Kafka, Virginia Woolf, Dylan Thomas, Dashiell Hammett, Iris Murdoch, Dennis Potter or the Venerable Bede. None of them began writing to lose weight or clarify the way they wanted to live. A lot of them did it to make money, but mainly it was because they felt they had something to say that could only be expressed on paper.

Look, generally there is just too much stuff – we need less, not more. In fact, never mind *writing* a book – a more useful exercise, to the greater benefit of mankind, would be to go through a bookshop and start chucking out books that should never have been written in the first place. Anyone want a list of those? By all means start with this one.

# Save yourself even more effort with the
## *Can't Be Arsed Agreeable Holiday Planner*

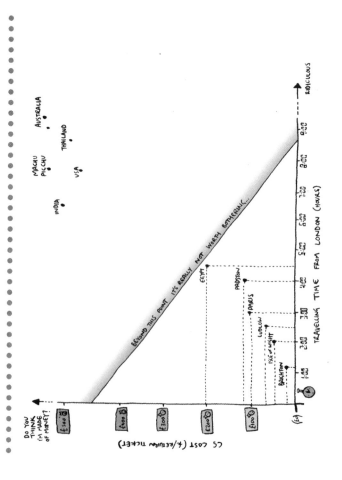

# Bibliography

In the course of researching this book there were many titles that I couldn't quite be arsed to get round to reading. Here is a short list of just some of the books that you really don't have to bother reading before you die...

*50 Fish To Catch Before You Die,* John Bailey, 2008.

*50 Places To See Before You Die & 50 Places That Are A Lot More Fun,* Nicholas Noyes, 2008.

*97 Things To Do Before You Finish High-School,* Steven Jenkins & Erika Stalder, 2007.

*100 Belgian Beers To Try Before You Die!,* Tim Webb & Joris Pattyn, 2008.

*100 Birds To See Before You Die,* Nick Baker, 2008.

*100 Things To Do Before You Die: Travel Events You Just Can't Miss,* Dave Freeman & Neil Teplica, 1999.

*101 Places To Have Sex Before You Die,* Marsha Normandy & Joseph St. James, 2008.

*101 Things To Buy Before You Die,* Charlotte Williamson & Maggie Davis, 2007.

*101 Things To Do Before You Die,* Richard Horne, 2004.

*101 Things To Do In Alabama Before You Up and Die,* Ellen Patrick, 2006.

*101 Things To Do In Florida Before You Up and Die,* Ellen Patrick, 2006.

# Bibliography

*101 Things To Do In Georgia Before You Up and Die*, Ellen Patrick, 2006.

*101 Things To Do In Louisiana Before You Up and Die*, Ellen Patrick, 2006.

*101 Things To Do In Mississippi Before You Up and Die*, Ellen Patrick, 2006.

*101 Things To Do In North Carolina Before You Up and Die*, Ellen Patrick, 2006.

*101 Things To Do In South Carolina Before You Up and Die*, Ellen Patrick, 2006.

*101 Things To Do in Tennessee Beofre You Up and Die*, Ellen Patrick, 2006.

*101 Things To Do In Virginia Before You Up and Die*, Ellen Patrick, 2006.

*101 Things You Should Do Before Going To Heaven*, Tom Winters & David Brodon, 2006.

*300 Beers To Try Before You Die*, Roger Protz, CAMRA, 2005.

*1000 Places To See Before You Die*, Patricia Schultz, 2003.

*1000 Places To See in the USA and Canada Before You Die*, Patricia Schultz, 2007.

*1001 Albums You Must Hear Before You Die*, Robert Dimery, 2005.

*1001 Books You Must Read Before You Die*, Peter Boxall, 2006.

*1001 Buildings You Must See Before You Die*, Mark Irving (ed.) 2007.

*1001 Classical Recordings You Must Hear Before You Die*, Matthew Rye, 2007.

*1001 Foods You Must Try Before You Die*, Theodora Sutcliffe, 2008.

*1001 Gardens You Must See Before You Die,* Rae Spencer-Jones, 2007.

*1001 Golf Holes You Must Play Before You Die,* Bradley S. Klein & Jeff Barr, 2005.

*1001 Historic Sites You Must See Before You Die,* Richard Cavendish, 2008.

*1001 Movies You Must See Before You Die,* Steven Jay Schneider, 2007.

*1001 Natural Wonders You Must See Before You Die,* Michael Bright, 2005.

*1001 Paintings You Must See Before You Die,* Stephen Farthing, 2006.

*1000 Recordings To Hear Before You Die,* Tom Moon, 2008.

*1001 Things You Should Know Before You Die,* Allan & Yvonne Ansdell, 2008.

*1001 Wines You Must Taste Before You Die,* Hugh Johnson & Neil Beckett, 2008.

*2,001 Things To Do Before You Die,* Dane Sherwood, 1997.

*Can't Be Arsed: 101 Things Not To Do Before You Die,* Richard Wilson, 2008.

*Do It Now: 1001 Things To Do Before You Check Out,* Gary W. Buffone, 2002.

*Eat This! 1001 Things To Eat Before You Diet,* Ian Jackman, 2007.

*Epic Spots: The Places You Must Skate Before You Die,* Thrasher Magazine, 2008.

*Fifty Places To Dive Before You Die: Diving Experts Share The World's Greatest Destinations,* Chris Santella, 2007.

*Fifty Places To Fly-Fish Before You Die, Fly-Fishing Experts Share The World's Greatest Destinations,* Chris Santella, 2004.

# Bibliography

*Fifty Places To Go Birding Before You Die: Birding Experts Share The World's Greatest Destinations,* Chris Santella, 2007.

*Fifty Places To Play Golf Before You Die: Golfing Experts Share The World's Greatest Destinations,* Chris Santella, 2005.

*Fifty Places To Sail Before You Die: Sailing Experts Share The World's Greatest Destinations,* Chris Santella, 2007.

*Five Secrets You Must Discover Before You Die,* John Izzo, 2007.

*F\*\*k That: 103 Things Not To Do Before You Die,* Sam Jordison, 2008.

*Stroke A Martian: And 99 Other Things To Do Before You Die,* New Scientist, 2005.

*Ten Fun Things To Do Before You Die,* Karol Jakowski, 2000.

*To Die For: 100 Gastronomic Experiences to Have Before You Die,* Stephen Downes, 2006.

*Unforgettable Islands To Escape To Before You Die,* Steve Davey & Marc Schlossman, 2007.

*Unforgettable Journeys To Take Before You Die,* Steve Watkins & Clare Jones, 2006.

*Unforgettable Places To See Before You Die,* Steve Davey, 2004.

*Unforgettable Things To Do Before You Die,* Steve Watkins & Clare Jones, 2005.

*Unforgettable Walks To Take Before You Die,* Steve Watkins & Clare Jones, 2008.

# Acknowledgements

· · · · · · · · · · · · · · · · · · · · · · · · · · · · · · · · · · ·

I couldn't have finished this book without my agent Jennifer Christie, who kept pointing out that I wouldn't get paid until I'd actually handed some stuff in.

Thanks also to my Editor Tom Bromley for his encouragement and hats off to him for trying to stick up for Bob Dylan.

Many thanks also to Paul Merton and all the other comedians who have helped me to pay my mortgage. Apologies to them for any jokes I may have stolen by accident.

Most of all thanks to my wife Stephanie for instinctively knowing which bits she was supposed to laugh at.